MRs BEETON'S

HEALTHY EATING

MAKING MORE OF VEGETABLES

Consultant Editor
Bridget Jones

WARD LOCK

A WARD LOCK BOOK

First published in the UK 1994
by Ward Lock
A Cassell Imprint
Villiers House
41/47 Strand
LONDON
WC2N 5JE

Edited by Jenni Fleetwood
Designed by Anne Fisher
Cover artwork by Angela Barnes
Inside artwork by Kevin Jones Associates

Distributed in the United States
by Sterling Publishing Co., Inc.
387 Park Avenue South, New York, NY 10016-8810

Distributed in Australia
by Capricorn Link (Australia) Pty Ltd
P.O. Box 665, Lane Cove, NSW 2066

British Library Cataloguing in Publication Data
The CIP data for this book is available
upon application to the British Library

ISBN 0-7063-7185-2

Typeset by Litho Link Ltd, Welshpool, Powys, Wales
Printed and bound in Spain by Cronion S.A. Barcelona

**Mrs Beeton's is a registered trademark
of Ward Lock Ltd**

CONTENTS

USEFUL WEIGHTS AND MEASURES

USING METRIC OR IMPERIAL MEASURES

Throughout the book, all weights and measures are given first in metric, then in Imperial. For example 100 g/4 oz, 150 ml/¼ pint or 15 ml/1 tbsp.

When following any of the recipes use either metric or Imperial – do not combine the two sets of measures as they are not interchangeable.

Weights The following chart lists some of the metric/Imperial weights that are used in the recipes.

METRIC	IMPERIAL
15 g	½ oz
25 g	1 oz
50 g	2 oz
75 g	3 oz
100 g	4 oz
150 g	5 oz
175 g	6 oz
200 g	7 oz
225 g	8 oz
250 g	9 oz
275 g	10 oz
300 g	11 oz
350 g	12 oz
375 g	13 oz
400 g	14 oz
425 g	15 oz
450 g	1 lb
575 g	1¼ lb
675 g	1½ lb
800 g	1¾ lb
900 g	2 lb
1 kg	2¼ lb
1.4 kg	3 lb
1.6 kg	3½ lb
1.8 kg	4 lb
2.25 kg	5 lb

Liquid Measures Millilitres (ml), litres and fluid ounces (fl oz) or pints are used.

METRIC	IMPERIAL
50 ml	2 fl oz
125 ml	4 fl oz
150 ml	¼ pint
300 ml	½ pint
450 ml	¾ pint
600 ml	1 pint

Spoon Measures Both metric and Imperial equivalents are given for all spoon measures, expressed as millilitres and teaspoons (tsp) or tablespoons (tbsp).

All spoon measures refer to British standard measuring spoons and the quantities given are always for level spoons.

Do not use ordinary kitchen cutlery instead of proper measuring spoons as they will hold quite different quantities.

METRIC	IMPERIAL
1.25 ml	¼ tsp
2.5 ml	½ tsp
5 ml	1 tsp
15 ml	1 tbsp

Length All linear measures are expressed in millimetres (mm), centimetres (cm) or metres (m) and inches or feet. The following list gives examples of typical conversions.

METRIC	IMPERIAL
5 mm	¼ inch
1 cm	½ inch
2.5 cm	1 inch
5 cm	2 inches
15 cm	6 inches
30 cm	12 inches (1 foot)

OVEN TEMPERATURES

Three alternatives are used: degrees Celsius (°C), degrees Fahrenheit (°F) and gas. The settings given are for conventional ovens. If you have a fan oven, adjust the temperature according to the manufacturer's instructions.

°C	°F	GAS
110	225	¼
120	250	½
140	275	1
150	300	2
160	325	3
180	350	4
190	375	5
200	400	6
220	425	7
230	450	8
240	475	9

MICROWAVE INFORMATION

The information given is for microwave ovens rated at 650-700 watts.

The following terms have been used for the microwave settings: High, Medium, Defrost and Low. For each setting, the power input is as follows: High = 100% power, Medium = 50% power, Defrost = 30% power and Low = 20% power.

All microwave notes and timings are for guidance only: always read and follow the manufacturer's instructions for your particular appliance. Remember to avoid putting any metal in the microwave and never operate the microwave empty.

NOTES FOR AMERICAN READERS

In America the standard 8 oz cup measure is used. When translating pints, and fractions of pints, remember that the U.S. pint is equal to 16 fl oz or 2 cups, whereas the Imperial pint is 20 fl oz.

Equivalent metric/American measures

METRIC/IMPERIAL	AMERICAN
Weights	
450 g/1 lb butter or margarine	*2 cups (4 sticks)*
100 g/4 oz grated cheese	*1 cup*
450 g/1 lb flour	*4 cups*
450 g/1 lb granulated sugar	*2 cups*
450 g/1 lb icing sugar	*3½ cups confectioners' sugar*
200 g/7 oz raw long-grain rice	*1 cup*
100 g/4 oz cooked long-grain rice	*1 cup*
100 g/4 oz fresh white breadcrumbs	*2 cups*
Liquid Measures	
150 ml/¼ pint	*⅔ cup*
300 ml/½ pint	*1¼ cups*
450 ml/¾ pint	*2 cups*
600 ml/1 pint	*2½ cups*
900 ml/1½ pints	*3¾ cups*
1 litre/1¾ pints	*4 cups (2 U.S. pints)*

Terminology Some useful American equivalents or substitutes for British ingredients are listed below:

BRITISH	AMERICAN
aubergine	eggplant
bicarbonate of soda	baking soda
biscuits	cookies, crackers
broad beans	fava or lima beans
chicory	endive
cling film	plastic wrap
cornflour	cornstarch
courgettes	zucchini
cream, single	cream, light
cream, double	cream, heavy
flour, plain	flour, all-purpose
frying pan	skillet
grill	broil/broiler
minced meat	ground meat
prawn	shrimp
shortcrust pastry	basic pie dough
spring onion	scallion
sultana	golden raisin
swede	rutabaga

INTRODUCTION

The vital role that vegetables play in a healthy diet is undisputed. Their long-established place on the British menu has moved ahead, with a contemporary approach advocating shorter cooking times and greater use of the variety of imported produce that is available.

The meat-and-two-veg tradition has been greatly criticized from all sides, with more emphasis being placed on pasta and rice. The increased dependence on convenience foods and the swing towards spending the minimum time on preparing and cooking everyday meals have also had an impact on traditional eating habits, yet the tradition of bulking out a modest portion of meat with ample quantities of vegetables, hot soup or generous portions of bread is entirely compatible with the healthy thinking behind much of today's dietary advice.

Vegetables and carbohydrate foods should provide the satisfying bulk in the diet. On a practical level, they enhance the appearance of protein foods such as fish, poultry and meat, and make them more palatable. In the context of balanced eating, vegetables provide essential vitamins and minerals as well as protein (particularly in the case of peas and beans) and valuable fibre. Fresh raw vegetables offer the greatest source of nutrients and fibre; the loss of nutrients can be kept to a minimum by preparing the vegetables just before cooking, cooking them only until they are tender and in as little water or other liquid as possible.

The chapters in this book bring together traditional and contemporary recipes for a broad range of vegetables, highlighting the versatility of these ingredients and the many ways in which they can be served to suit all types of meals. They may be the key ingredients on the menu, complement the main dish or extend the protein food in a colourful and exciting recipe. The basic information on buying and preparing vegetables, along with the recipes, indicate the possibilities.

All food can play a role in a healthy diet. Healthy eating means eating a wide variety of foods in the correct proportions, cooked by different methods. It is wrong to think of some foods as being 'healthy' and others as being 'unhealthy'; it is more correct and practical to divide foods into groups according to the proportions in which they should be eaten.

Fat plays an important role in the diet as a source of energy and nutrients – it must not be eliminated but must be limited. Of the total energy intake, no more than 35 per cent should be derived from fat. Saturated fats should not provide more than 10 per cent of the energy intake. The majority of the fat consumed should be based on monounsaturated sources (up to 17 per cent), leaving a recommended maximum of 8 per cent for the polyunsaturated fats. Animal fats and some fats from vegetable sources (notably coconut fat) are saturated. High fat foods – whether of animal or vegetable origin – should not form a large part of the diet. Butter, margarine, cream, full-fat cheeses, oils and fatty meats or products rich in these ingredients should be eaten in moderation or set aside for occasional consumption only.

Sugar, its products and other sweeteners, such as honey, should also be limited in the diet. Eating large amounts of sugar or very sweet foods encourages tooth decay. Eating too many sweet foods may mean that other more nutritious foods are not eaten in sufficient quantities or it can result in problems of overweight or obesity.

On the positive side, fruit, vegetables, starchy foods and foods which provide fibre should make up a large proportion of the diet. The starchy foods should provide the majority of the energy requirements, fibre should be obtained from cereal origins as well as from vegetable sources, and fresh fruit and vegetables are also important as a source of certain vitamins. We should aim to include five different pieces of fruit or vegetables in the diet every day – this includes any portions of fresh fruit, cooked vegetables, salads and significant portions of salad in chunky sandwiches.

Alongside the choice of foods in the diet, the cooking methods used are important. There should be emphasis on regularly eating some raw fruit and vegetables. Avoid frequently cooking by methods which call for adding significant amounts of additional fat – deep frying is the most obvious method which should be set aside for rare use; shallow frying and stir frying should use the minimum of extra fat, and grilling without extra fat is the better option on a day-to-day basis. Overcooking vegetables by boiling them in large amounts of water must be avoided as nutrients are lost to the cooking water. Never add bicarbonate of soda to the cooking water for vegetables as this destroys vitamin C.

Following a healthy eating plan does not mean analyzing every meal nor anxiously assessing everything consumed over 24 hours: the correct approach is to consider meals over a few days or a week and in the long term.

The recipes in this book have been selected as much for ease of preparation as for their role in a balanced diet. The emphasis throughout is on including a good range of foods, recipes and cooking methods in the diet, at the same time recognizing practical considerations, such as the cost of food and the use of labour-saving appliances or modern food storage facilities. A guide to food value is included with each recipe, providing information on the protein, carbohydrate, fat, fibre and energy value (kcals). As well as using this information for an occasional check on the content of your diet, you may find it helpful to compare different recipes or to compare the food value of home cooking with information on bought ingredients and cooked products.

NUTRITION AND DIET

A basic understanding of nutrition leads to an awareness of the food we eat in relation to its use by the body and, consequently, to an appreciation of the importance of eating a balanced diet.

Food is the essential fuel for life, maintaining the body as well as building and repairing it. Foods are made up of a combination of different nutrients and, as the body digests the food, these nutrients are released and utilized. General guidelines are provided regarding the nutritional needs of the population; however, individual requirements vary. Factors that influence any one person's dietary needs include gender, age, build, lifestyle and health.

BALANCED DIET

A balanced diet provides all the essential nutrients and sufficient energy to meet an individual's needs and to maintain a healthy body weight without causing obesity. In young people, the diet must also include sufficient nutrients to sustain growth. Nutritional requirements relating to pregnancy, lactation, illness and special conditions should be provided by a doctor and/or dietician.

A balanced diet should include a wide selection of different types of foods, prepared and cooked in a variety of ways. Fresh foods and 'whole' foods are important in providing a balanced variety of nutrients. Raw and lightly cooked fruit and vegetables are also essential.

In general terms, the carbohydrate and vegetable content of the diet should dominate the protein and fat. A diet that lacks carbohydrate, fruit and vegetables is likely to have too high a fat content and to be lacking in fibre. Fibre, from vegetable and cereal sources, is also a vital ingredient for a balanced diet.

BASIC GUIDE TO NUTRIENTS

Protein
Used by the body for growth and repair, protein foods are composed of amino acids, in various amounts and combinations according to the food. There are eight specific amino acids which are an essential part of an adult's diet as they cannot be manufactured by the body from other foods; an additional one is necessary for young children, to sustain their rapid growth. In addition, nine other amino acids are widely available in protein foods, although a high intake of these is not vital as the human body can manufacture them if they are not adequately supplied by the diet.

8

The quality of any one protein food is determined by the number and proportion of amino acids it contains. Animal foods have a higher biological value than vegetable foods because they provide all the essential amino acids. Generally, no single vegetable food provides all the essential amino acids and they are not present in the proportions best suited to the human body. There are, however, important exceptions to this rule; certain non-animal foods are excellent sources of protein, notably soya beans, some types of nut and mycoprotein (quorn). Other beans and pulses, nuts and cereals are also excellent sources of good-quality protein. Since the amino acid content of vegetable foods varies, by mixing different foods and eating them in sufficient amounts, the necessary types and quantities of amino acids may be obtained.

As amino acids are not stored in a digestible form in the body, a regular supply is essential. This is most easily obtained from a mixture of animal and vegetable sources; if fish, poultry and meat are not eaten, then it is vital that a broad selection of vegetable sources and dairy foods are included to provide sufficient quantities of amino acids.

Carbohydrates
These are the energy-giving foods and may be divided into two main categories: starches and sugars. Starch is obtained from vegetables, cereals, some nuts and under-ripe bananas; sugar is found in fruit (including ripe bananas), honey, molasses and cane sugar.

Carbohydrates in the form of starch, known as complex carbohydrates, should form a significant proportion of the diet. For example, they should be eaten in larger quantities than protein foods, such as meat, poultry and fish. The sugar content of the diet should be limited.

If the diet is deficient in carbohydrates, the body will break down other foods to supply energy, eventually including proteins which have a more valuable role to play.

Fibre
At one time referred to as roughage, fibre is a complex carbohydrate which is not totally digested and absorbed by the body; however, it is vital as a carrier of moisture and waste products through the digestive system.

Fibre is obtained from cereals and vegetables. Good sources are wholegrain rice, oats, wholemeal flour and its products. Sources of vegetable fibre include beans and pulses, some types of fruit, as well as vegetables.

Raw and lightly cooked foods (where appropriate) generally provide more fibre than well-cooked foods; similarly more refined foods offer less fibre than wholefoods and unrefined ingredients.

Fats
Fat and oils provide energy as well as being important sources of certain vitamins and fatty acids. They may be loosely divided into saturated fats and unsaturated fats. Unsaturated fats may be further grouped into polyunsaturated and monounsaturated, depending on their chemical compositions. Although

the majority of fatty foods contain both saturated and unsaturated fats, as a general rule animal sources have a higher proportion of saturated fats and vegetable sources are richer in unsaturates.

The recommended fat intake is calculated as a percentage of the total energy value of the diet. The energy value (in calories or joules) of fat eaten should be no more than 35% of the total energy intake with the major proportion of fat in the diet being the unsaturated type.

It is important to remember that young children (under five years of age) should not follow low-fat diets. Although their meals should not contain high proportions of fatty foods (fried foods, chips, high-fat snacks), their fat intake should not be limited by the use of skimmed milk, low-fat cheese and so on.

Vitamins

Although each of the vitamins has specific functions within the body, they also play vital roles in regulating metabolism, helping to repair tissues and assisting in the conversion of carbohydrates and fats into energy. Vitamin deficiency results in general poor health as well as certain specific illnesses.

Vitamins fall into two groups; fat-soluble and water-soluble. Fat-soluble vitamins include A, D, E and K; water-soluble vitamins include C and B-group vitamins. Fat-soluble vitamins can be stored by the body, whereas any excess of the water-soluble type is passed out. This means that a regular supply of water-soluble vitamins is essential and that an excess is unlikely to be harmful. Conversely, the fat-soluble vitamins which are stored in the body should not be consumed to excess as this can result in a condition known as hypervitaminosis. It is important to remember that an excess can be dangerous when taking vitamin supplements, or when eating a very high proportion of foods which are particularly rich in any one (or more) of the fat-soluble vitamins.

Vitamin A Found in fish liver oils, liver, kidney, dairy produce and eggs, vitamin A is important to prevent night blindness. It also contributes to the general health of the eyes and to the condition of the skin. Carotene, found in carrots and yellow or dark green vegetables such as peppers and spinach, can be converted into vitamin A in the body.

If the diet is excessively rich in vitamin A, or supplements are taken for a prolonged period, it is possible for stores to build up to toxic levels in the human liver.

B-group Vitamins This is a large group of water-soluble vitamins, linked because of their importance and use in the body. They play vital roles in promoting chemical reactions, in the release of energy from food and in the efficient functioning of the nervous system. They are essential for general good health and deficiency diseases occur comparatively quickly if these vitamins are missing from the diet.

Thiamin (vitamin B1), riboflavin (vitamin B2), vitamin B12, vitamin B6 (pyridoxine), nicotinic acid, folate, pantothenic acid and biotin are all included in this group (or complex) and each has its own particular characteristics.

In general, meat, offal, dairy produce, and cereals are good sources of B-group vitamins. Some of these vitamins are destroyed by prolonged cooking, notably thiamin, and long exposure to sunlight destroys riboflavin which is found in milk. Refined flour and bread are fortified with thiamin to meet natural levels in comparable wholemeal products. Breakfast cereals are also enriched with, or naturally rich in, B-group vitamins.

Vitamin C or Ascorbic Acid A water-soluble vitamin, this cannot be stored in the body, therefore a regular supply is essential. The main function of this vitamin is to maintain healthy connective tissue (the cell-structure within the body) and healthy blood. It also plays an important role in the healing of wounds. A deficiency can lead to susceptibility to infections.

Vitamin C is found in fresh and frozen vegetables, notably peppers and green vegetables, and in fruit, particularly blackcurrants and citrus fruit. Many fruit juices and drinks are fortified with vitamin C. Potatoes are also a valuable supply; although they are not a rich source, when eaten regularly and in quantity they make an important contribution to a healthy diet.

Vitamin C is the most easily destroyed of all vitamins and may be affected by light, heat, staleness, exposure to air and overcooking. The vitamin is also destroyed by alkaline substances, such as bicarbonate of soda.

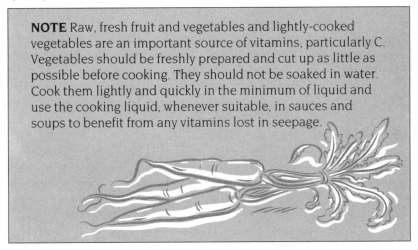

NOTE Raw, fresh fruit and vegetables and lightly-cooked vegetables are an important source of vitamins, particularly C. Vegetables should be freshly prepared and cut up as little as possible before cooking. They should not be soaked in water. Cook them lightly and quickly in the minimum of liquid and use the cooking liquid, whenever suitable, in sauces and soups to benefit from any vitamins lost in seepage.

Vitamin D Essential in promoting calcium absorption, a deficiency will result in an inadequate supply of calcium being made available for building and repairing bones and teeth. A diet which is too rich in vitamin D can result in excessive calcium absorption and storage which can be damaging, so supplements should only be taken on medical advice.

Vitamin D is manufactured by the body from the action of sunlight on the skin – this is the primary source for most adults. The vitamin is naturally present in cod liver oil and oily fish such as herrings, mackerel, salmon and sardines. Eggs contain vitamin D, and it can also be manufactured from vegetable sources. Some foods, such as margarine, are fortified with vitamin D.

Vitamin E This vitamin is found in small amounts in most foods and the better sources include vegetable oils, eggs and cereals (especially wheatgerm).

Its role in the body is not clearly established, although unsubstantiated claims are made about its contribution to fertility and its role in improving circulation.

Vitamin K Widely found in vegetables and cereals, this vitamin can be manufactured in the body. Vitamin K contributes towards normal blood clotting. Deficiency is rare, due to a ready supply being available in a mixed diet.

A broad mixed diet, including plenty of raw and lightly cooked fruit and vegetables as well as animal and dairy foods, is likely to provide an adequate supply of vitamins. The value of fresh foods, dairy produce, bread and cereals is obvious. Deficiency can occur in restricted diets where meat and poultry are not eaten and corresponding levels of vitamins are not taken from dairy products or cereals. Those following a vegan diet are most vulnerable, and a diet free of animal products is not recommended.

Minerals

Minerals and trace elements are essential for a healthy body as they play important roles in metabolic processes relating to to the nervous system, glands, muscle control and the supply of water. They are only required in minute quantities and a well balanced diet containing plenty of fresh and whole foods should provide an adequate supply. Mineral supplements should only be taken on medical advice as overdoses can upset metabolism.

Iron An essential constituent of red blood cells and important in muscles, iron can be stored in the body. The diet must maintain the store as, if it becomes depleted, anaemia can result. An adequate supply of iron is especially important during menstruation and pregnancy, as both use up the iron supply.

Found in meat, offal and green vegetables, such as spinach, and eggs, the iron in meat and offal is the most readily absorbed; it is less easily utilized from vegetable sources. The availability of vitamin C is important to promote iron absorption; other factors, such as the presence of tannin, can impair absorption.

Calcium Important in building and maintaining healthy teeth and bones, as well as for normal blood clotting, muscle function and a healthy nervous system, calcium is obtained from milk, cheese, bread, fortified flour and vegetables. The calcium found in milk and dairy produce is likely to be more easily absorbed than that in green vegetables or whole grains (although the system can adjust to utilizing the mineral from less ready sources) and an adequate supply of vitamin D is necessary for efficient calcium absorption.

Phosphorus Along with calcium, this is valuable for bones and teeth. It is widely distributed in food and deficiency is unknown in man.

Potassium, Chlorine and Sodium These play an important role in the balance of body fluids and they are essential for muscle and nerve function. Sodium and chlorine are added to food in the form of salt; sodium is found naturally in meat and milk, and it is added to bread, cereal products and manufactured foods. Potassium is found naturally in meat, vegetables and milk.

Trace Elements These are required by the body in very small amounts and include iodine, fluorine, magnesium, zinc, manganese, cobalt, selenium, molybdenum and chromium. An adequate supply of trace elements is almost always found in the diet and deficiency is extremely rare. Unprescribed supplements should be avoided as they can be detrimental to health.

SPECIFIC NEEDS

Most people have particular dietary needs at some time during their life, if only as babies or young children.

Babies
Breast milk is the ideal food for young babies as it provides all the nutrients they require for the first few months of life. Even if this method of feeding is not continued in the long term, it is a very good idea to breast-feed a baby for the first few days, as valuable antibodies are passed from the mother to help the baby fight infection in the early months.

Bottle-fed babies should be given one of the manufactured milk formulas. These should be prepared exactly according to the manufacturer's instructions or according to the health visitor's or doctor's advice.

Regular checks on the baby's progress are important and any problems should be brought to professional attention immediately.

The weaning process varies from infant to infant; however, between the ages of four to six months a baby should be ready to try a little solid food. By eighteen months, the infant should be able to cope with a mixed diet based on adult foods, following general guidelines for balanced eating. Milk is still an important supplement during this time of rapid growth.

Toddlers and Young Children
Fads and eating difficulties are common in young children, who are too busy discovering the world around them to concentrate for the length of time necessary to learn about meals. Since toddlers and young children are quickly satisfied, it is important that they are introduced to good eating habits and that their meals are nutritious; sweet or fatty snacks are to be avoided and bread, milk, vegetables, fruit, cheese and other valuable foods should be introduced. New foods should be presented in small amounts along with familiar ingredients. Milk is still an important source of nutrients, particularly for difficult eaters.

Providing a meal-time routine and making the process of eating a pleasure is all-important. Children should not be encouraged to play with food, but they should look forward to eating it. Small, frequent yet regular meals, are ideal: in theory, these occasions should be relaxed, free of distractions from the business of eating, and traumatic scenes relating to food rejection should be avoided.

School Children

Fast-growing and active children need a highly nutritious diet, so the substitution of sweets, fatty snacks, sweet drinks and sticky cakes for meals should be avoided. These types of foods should be rare treats.

Breakfasts and packed lunches need special attention. The first meal of the day should be nutritious and provide sufficient energy to keep the child on the move until lunchtime: bread, cereals and milk, eggs and fruit are all practical and useful foods. Raw vegetables, semi-sweet biscuits and crackers are practical mid-morning snack foods but they should not spoil the appetite for lunch. Packed lunches, if eaten, should contain a variety of foods – bread, salad vegetables, some form of protein and a piece of fruit. If a packed lunch is the norm, tea and an early supper are important meals.

As a general guide, every meal should provide growing children with a good balance of valuable nutrients, and additional milk drinks (whole or semi-skimmed) are excellent sources of the calcium which is so important for strong teeth and bones, as well as other nutrients. Sweet foods and confectionery should be avoided as they cause tooth decay and can lead to obesity; similarly, fatty cooking methods and high-fat foods should not be a regular feature in the diet. The importance of fibre, raw fruit and vegetables must be stressed.

Adolescents and Teenagers

This group also requires a highly nutritious, energy-packed diet, but unfortunately, young people are particularly prone to food fads and fashions and it can be difficult to get a teenager to eat a balanced diet. While it is essential to provide all the necessary nutrients, it is important to avoid obesity in this group. Reduced-calorie diets are not recommended, but over-eating must be controlled and the types of food eaten should be carefully monitored.

During this period of rapid growth and development, adopting an active lifestyle and participating in regular exercise is as important as eating well. Young people in this age group should be encouraged to take an interest in nutrition, food and the relationship between a balanced diet, health and fitness.

Parents should try to pass on an understanding of food shopping, meal planning and food preparation, together with an appreciation of the positive benefits of a good diet. This is particularly important for young people who are about to embark on their first experience of living alone and catering for themselves.

Pregnancy and Lactation

A woman should pay special attention to diet during pregnancy as she will need to provide sufficient nutrients and energy for her own needs as well as those of the growing baby. The nutritional requirements continue after birth and during lactation, when the mother is feeding the new baby. The doctor or clinic should provide dietary advice, recommending supplements as necessary.

The mother's responsibility is to ensure that her diet is varied, with emphasis on foods rich in minerals, vitamins and energy. Sweets, chocolates and foods which satisfy without offering nutritional benefit should be avoided in favour of fruit, vegetables, dairy produce, bread and protein foods.

Elderly People

Problems relating to nutrition and the elderly are often linked to social factors. The cost and effort of eating well can deter some elderly people from shopping for a variety of foods and therefore from cooking fresh ingredients. Although many elderly people are extremely active, others may have physical difficulty in shopping or spending long periods standing to prepare meals; in this case help should be sought with planning a practical diet. Equally, dental problems restrict some elderly people from eating well and these can, and should, be overcome by visiting a dentist.

Hot, solid meals are important, particularly in winter. Some elderly people get through the day by eating lots of snacks and this can be detrimental to health; cakes, biscuits and favourite puddings may be pleasant and comforting but they do not constitute a balanced diet. The appetite is often reduced, particularly as the person becomes less active, so meals that are small must contain a high proportion of valuable nutrients. Wholemeal bread, dairy products and cereals with milk are all practical snacks.

The pleasure often disappears from eating when meals are lonely occasions and the palate is not as efficient as it once was. Special centres and meal services exist and these should be used, not only by those who are prevented from cooking for themselves by physical limitations, but also by all who need the company and contact that such services offer.

USING THE FOOD VALUES WITH THE RECIPES

All recipes (except stocks) include a guide to the content of key nutrients: protein, carbohydrate, fat and fibre.

- Where less rich alternatives are given for high-fat foods, the food values are based on the lighter ingredient. For example if an ingredients list includes either cream or fromage frais, the food values reflect the latter.
- Values are based on very low-fat fromage frais where applicable.
- Optional ingredients are not included in food values.
- Total values and values per portion are provided. The values per portion relate to the number of servings suggested at the end of the recipe unless otherwise stated. Where a range of servings is given, the number used in the calculation is given in brackets in the chart.
- Quantities are expressed in grammes (g) and rounded up to the nearest whole figure. Where a value is less than 1g, a dash indicates that the content of that nutrient is negligible in the context of this information.

A GUIDE TO VEGETABLES

Variety and quality are all-important in the selection and use of vegetables. This book offers traditional and contemporary ideas to ensure that, whatever their role, the vegetables will complement the rest of the menu.

BUYING VEGETABLES

Although most vegetables are on sale all year, it is still worth taking advantage of locally grown produce in season, both for flavour and economy. Look out for home-grown produce in supermarkets and take advantage of any local market gardens and farms. Remember, too, that markets are an excellent place to shop for value – in some rural areas they can be the best place to buy really fresh produce.

Whatever and wherever you buy, always look for good-quality produce. Vegetables should look fresh – firm, crisp and bright. Avoid limp, yellowing and wrinkled produce; onions that are soft or sprouting; and items that have been excessively trimmed. Do not buy green potatoes as they are inedible; this should be brought to the attention of the seller.

The fact that vegetables have been cleaned is not necessarily an indication of their quality – for example, vegetables that have a certain amount of earth on them or retain their leaves are often better quality than thoroughly washed, trimmed and prepacked items.

When buying packs of vegetables always check that they are not sweating, with moisture inside the bag causing rapid deterioration in quality. Turn items over, feel them and inspect them for soft spots or bad patches.

Storing

Vegetables should be used as fresh as possible. The majority of vegetables should be stored in the refrigerator: salad vegetables should be polythene-wrapped or stored in the salad drawer.

Carrots, parsnips and similar vegetables soon deteriorate if they are stored in polythene bags, so thick paper bags are the best wrapping in the salad drawer. Similarly, mushrooms go off quickly if they are stored in polythene. Green vegetables and cauliflower should be stored in polythene bags.

Potatoes should be stored only if suitable conditions are available; that is a cool, dry place where the tubers may be kept in a thick brown paper bag to exclude all light. They should not be stored in warm, light, moist conditions for any length of time. So only buy large polythene bags of potatoes if you can use them within a few days.

As a general rule, buy little and often for best quality and food value.

Frozen Vegetables

Frozen vegetables are excellent quality, in terms of food value as well as flavour. They are also easy to prepare at home. Take advantage of pick-your-own farms or farm shops if you do not grow your own vegetables, and freeze only good quality produce which is freshly picked and processed as quickly as possible.

COOKING METHODS

British cooking has been given a bad name by the characteristic overboiling of vegetables, rendering high-quality produce unpalatable and lacking in nutrients. Happily, attitudes are changing and a far broader range of cooking methods is now commonly used, with shorter cooking times and greater appreciation of the value of raw vegetables, for their texture and flavour as well as for their food value. Flavourings have become more adventurous and salt, once added automatically to every pan of boiling vegetables, is now very much a matter of personal choice.

Boiling This is an easy and practical cooking method for many vegetables including potatoes, carrots, swedes, parsnips, beans, cauliflower and cabbage. However, it is important that the boiling process is only long enough to make the vegetables tender.

There are two methods of boiling. The first involves covering vegetables with water, which is then brought to the boil. The heat is then reduced and the pan covered so that the water just boils. For the second method, a comparatively small amount of water is brought to the boil, the vegetables are added and are cooked more fiercely with or without a lid on the pan. This takes less time.

The first method is used for potatoes, swedes and similar vegetables which require to be covered with liquid to make them tender in the shortest possible time. The liquid from cooking may be used for sauces, gravy, or in soups.

The second method is suitable for quick-cooking vegetables such as cabbage, green beans, Brussels sprouts and cauliflower. Once the vegetables are added to the pan, the liquid should be brought back to the boil quickly, then the heat controlled so that the cooking is fairly rapid. Cooking times will vary, depending on the vegetables.

Salt may be added to the cooking water. This is a matter of personal choice but the water should not be heavily salted.

Never add bicarbonate of soda to the cooking water for green vegetables. In the days when vegetables were regularly overcooked, this was regarded as a good way of preserving the colour; however it destroys the vitamin C content of the food and should be avoided.

Stewing and Braising Ratatouille is one of the best-known, classic vegetable stews. Stewing and braising are used for vegetables which require moderate to lengthy cooking. or which benefit from a moist cooking method. They are also used to combine vegetable flavours and create a mixed vegetable dish.

Celery, fennel, cucumber and carrots are typical examples of vegetables that respond well to braising, with the addition of a little onion, some stock or wine and herbs. The braising process should be fairly slow so that the vegetables are tender throughout. The cooking juices are either reduced or thickened, then poured over the vegetables to serve.

Steaming This is a good, plain method which gives results similar to boiling. Nutrients are lost from the vegetables by seepage via the steam into the water below. To conserve as much food value as possible steam vegetables over a main dish such as a stew so that the nutrients are retained.

Although a perforated container is usually used, vegetables that require light cooking, such as courgettes, may be steamed in a dish, on a plate over a saucepan of water or wrapped in foil.

The flavour of some vegetables is heightened by steaming rather than boiling. Cauliflower, broccoli and cabbage are examples of this.

Frying Shallow frying, under the guise of sautéing, is a popular method for vegetables that require little cooking. Courgettes are often cooked by this method. The thinly cut vegetables are tossed in a little butter or oil over moderate to high heat.

Deep frying is not a practical way of cooking many vegetables but it is used for potato chips and for making fritters or vegetable croquettes. In the latter case, the portions of vegetable are protected by a coating, such as batter.

Stir Frying A comparatively modern method for Western cooks, this is suitable for most vegetables. The results are crisp, flavoursome and colourful. Many stir-fried vegetables are ideal for grilled dishes but are not the best accompaniment for casseroles or roasts.

Grilling This method is not often used for vegetables other than mushrooms or tomatoes. However, courgettes, aubergines and peppers may be grilled.

Microwave Cooking Microwave cooking is excellent for the majority of vegetables, particularly when small to medium quantities are cooked. The feature on microwave cooking on page 114 gives detailed information. Here are a few reminders:

- Never add salt before cooking.
- Cook vegetables with a small amount of water or liquid.
- Use a covered microwave-proof container or roasting bag, closed loosely to allow steam to escape.
- Arrange tougher areas, such as stalks, towards the outside of a dish, where they receive most energy.
- Turn and rearrange vegetables at least once during cooking.
- Spinach, peas, French beans, cauliflower florets, new potatoes, Jerusalem and globe artichokes are just a few examples of vegetables which cook very well in the microwave.
- Less successful vegetables include celery (unless as part of a dish), old carrots in chunks, large quantities of 'boiled' potatoes – particularly for mashing – and larger quantities of green cabbage.

A-Z OF
POPULAR VEGETABLES

ARTICHOKES

Globe At their best and least expensive during late summer, these are the flower buds of a large thistle. They should be thoroughly washed and drained. Trim off loose leaves around the base of the head. Snip off the ends of the leaves and the top of the head. Place in acidulated water to prevent discoloration and cook promptly in boiling salted water with lemon juice added. Allow 25-45 minutes, depending on size. To check if the artichokes are cooked, pull off one of the base leaves: it should come away easily. Drain well and cool.

Separate the leaves slightly to reveal the group of leaves that form the central part of the artichoke. Pull these out to reveal the 'choke', a cushion of fine hairs seated in the centre of the vegetable. Use a teaspoon to scrape the choke away carefully, leaving a pad of pale, tender flesh known as the bottom, base or fond. Trim off the stalk so that the artichoke sits neatly and fill the centre with an oil and vinegar dressing or a stuffing.

Like asparagus, artichokes are eaten with the fingers. Each leaf is pulled off individually and the small portion of pale flesh at the base dipped in dressing before being eaten. The rest of the tough leaf is discarded.

Artichoke bottoms (or fonds) are regarded as a delicacy and frequently form the basis of more sophisticated dishes. If only the artichoke bottoms are required, the leaves, chokes and stalks may be removed and the artichoke bottoms carefully peeled before being cooked in boiling water until tender.

Jerusalem These look like small, knobbly new potatoes, but have a delicate nutty flavour. They should be scrubbed and peeled or cooked with the peel left on. Jerusalem artichokes discolour quickly, so should be placed in acidulated water. Boil them for 10-15 minutes until tender or cook by steaming. They may be served gratinéed, with a crumb topping, mashed, coated in sauce, tossed in melted butter or sliced and topped with cheese, then grilled. They also make good soup.

ASPARAGUS

Although greengrocers have supplies throughout the year, home-grown asparagus is a summer vegetable, ready in May and June. Look for bright, firm but slim spears that are not woody. On larger spears, make sure that there is a good length of tender green stalk once the tougher end is trimmed. Allow 6-8 spears per portion.

Trip off the woody ends and scrape or peel any remaining tough spear ends. Tie the asparagus in bundles. Cook them in a special asparagus pan or stand them in a saucepan of boiling water, with the tender tips exposed. Tent with foil and simmer for about 15 minutes, or until tender. The tips will steam while the stalks cook in the simmering water.

Alternatively, asparagus may be steamed over boiling water on a rack in a wok or on a wire rack over boiling water in a roasting tin, with the tips towards the outside of the wok or tin so that they do not overcook.

Serve with melted butter poured over. The trimmings may be used to flavour soups or sauces.

AUBERGINES

Also known as eggplants (in America) and brinjals (in India), these vegetables have pale, tender but firm flesh. The shiny skins are usually purple, although white varieties are also available. They should be firm and shiny outside, with a bright green calyx. Aubergines are cooked in a wide variety of ways: they may be stewed in ratatouille; cubed and grilled on skewers; braised with meat or poultry; roasted and mashed to make a dip; stuffed and baked; sliced, fried and layered with meat in moussaka; or spiced in a variety of Indian or Mediterranean dishes.

Since the flesh can be rather bitter, aubergine flesh should be salted and allowed to stand in a colander or sieve over a bowl for 15-30 minutes before use. This process, which is also sometimes used for cucumbers, is known as *degorging*.

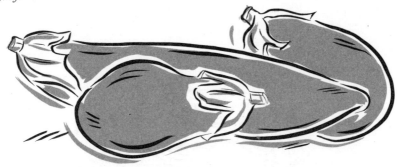

BEANS

Broad Available from early spring through to autumn, broad beans are best when young and small. Allow about 225 g / 8 oz pods per person, selecting firm plump pods with a good green colour. Shrivelled, blackened or largely empty pods are not a good buy. Equally, very large hard pods yield tough old beans.

Shell the broad beans and cook them in boiling water for 5-15 minutes. depending on their age and your personal taste. Add a sprig of summer savory to the cooking water if liked. Serve the beans with butter and pepper. They are excellent with diced cooked ham or crisp grilled bacon, or they may be sauced with Hollandaise sauce or soured cream.

French These require little preparation. Buy bright, firm beans which are not damaged or shrivelled. Trim off their ends and wash them well. Add to a pan of boiling water and cook for 2-10 minutes, depending on size and use. A crunchy result can quickly be achieved if the beans are very slim.

Serve French beans topped with butter or fried breadcrumbs. Chopped hard-boiled egg and chopped parsley is another popular topping.

Lightly cooked and cooled, these beans are good in salads. They may be stir fried.

Runner These are best freshly picked. It is usually necessary to remove the strings, or trim these beans down both sides, before cooking.

Some varieties do not need stringing. Avoid very large beans or any that have shrivelled.

Slice the beans at an angle into long thin pieces, add these to a saucepan of boiling water and cook for 3-10 minutes, depending on taste. About 5 minutes is average; any longer and the beans become soft. Toss with butter and serve freshly cooked.

BEAN SPROUTS

These are usually mung beans, although a variety of dried beans may be sprouted. Bean sprouts provide a useful amount of protein and are therefore ideal for adding to vegetable stir fries which contain little meat or fish.

The bean sprouts should be rinsed and drained, then cooked very briefly – stir frying for 3 minutes or less is the best method. The bean sprouts may be added to sauced mixtures and braised for 1-2 minutes, but avoid overcooking them or they will become limp and unpleasant.

BEETROOT

Do not peel raw beetroot before boiling. Simply wash away dirt and twist off the leaves above stalk level. Put the beetroot in a large saucepan with water to cover. Add some salt, if liked. Bring to the boil, lower the heat and simmer, covered, for 45-60 minutes for small to medium young beetroot. Larger, older vegetables can take up to 1-2 hours to cook but these are not often sold. Beetroot is cooked when it feels tender and the skin rubs off easily.

Drain off the cooking water and replace it with cold water to cover the beetroot. Working under water while the beetroot is still hot, rub off the skins. These should slip off easily with their stalks. Place the peeled beetroot in a dish, cover and leave until cool.

Beetroot may be served hot with fried breadcrumbs and chopped onion. It combines well with other vegetables in hot bakes, or it may be allowed to cool before being used in salads or served with soured cream or fromage frais.

Beetroot may also be sliced or preserved whole in vinegar. It is a traditional accompaniment for cold roast meats. The uncooked vegetable is also used to make a delicious soup, known as borsch.

BROCCOLI

The two main types are sprouting broccoli, with long stalks, a few leaves and small heads in purple or pale green, and calabrese with larger heads and shorter stalks. The stalks on young sprouting broccoli are tender when cooked and may be included as part of the vegetable; discard slightly older stalks.

Broccoli should be washed and trimmed, then broken if the heads are large. Cook in a saucepan of boiling water. Tender young sprouting broccoli cooks quite quickly and will be tender after 3-5 minutes but larger heads may require 10-15 minutes. Broccoli may also be steamed or stir fried, and makes an excellent soup.

Serve plain with butter or coated with a sauce, such as cheese sauce. Broken into small florets, broccoli may be cooked in a little olive oil with garlic and onion for tossing with pasta and serving with grated Parmesan cheese.

Broccoli is useful as a filling for pies, with chicken or fish, and it also makes a first class pancake filling.

BRUSSELS SPROUTS

This winter vegetable is one of the traditional accompaniments to roast turkey. Look for small firm sprouts which are slightly shiny and green. Avoid very loose, yellowing or insect-nibbled sprouts.

Wash the vegetables thoroughly. Cut a cross in the stalk end of larger ones so that they cook evenly. Add to boiling water and cook for 5-10 minutes.

Small, young sprouts may be steamed; halved sprouts may be stir fried. Cooked sprouts may be served plain, tossed with cooked chestnuts or mixed with browned blanched almonds.

CABBAGE

There are many varieties, the key differences being that they may be hard or loose-packed. The following are some of the varieties most commonly sold in Britain:

White Cabbage A hard creamy-white to pale green cabbage with tightly packed leaves.

Red Cabbage Resembles white cabbage but has dark red leaves.

Savoy Cabbage A large cabbage with a neat firm heart and slightly crinkly leaves.

Winter Cabbage A term used for cabbage with a firm heart and looser outer leaves, similar to Savoy but without the characteristic crinkly, deeply veined leaves.

Spring Green The new growth of loose leaves which do not have a heart.

There are many cooking methods for cabbage; all types may also be eaten raw. For salads, white and red cabbage are the most popular; they are also ideal for stir frying or braising. Red cabbage is also suitable for pickling in vinegar and white cabbage is traditionally salted to make sauerkraut.

Green cabbages may be boiled, steamed or stir fried. Individual leaves may be blanched until soft, then stuffed and braised. Shredded green cabbage may be blanched, drained, then deep fried and tossed in sugar and soy sauce to be served Chinese style as 'seaweed'.

Wedges of cabbage heart may be steamed or braised. Shredded cabbage may be combined with rice in risottos or added to soups.

To boil cabbage, add the trimmed leaves to the minimum of boiling water, pressing them down well. Cover the pan tightly and cook quickly for 3-7 minutes, according to taste. Drain and roughly chop the cabbage before tossing it with butter and pepper.

Steaming times vary according to the method of preparation: if the cabbage is cut in chunks allow up to 15 minutes. Braised cabbage may be cooked for anything from 15 minutes to 1½ hours (for red cabbage cooked with onions and apples).

CARROTS

Young, or baby, carrots have the best flavour. Look out for firm, unblemished carrots, preferably sold in bundles with leaves. If you do buy carrots prepacked in polythene, check that they are not wet from condensation; in damp conditions, they deteriorate very rapidly.

Young carrots do not require peeling; a good scrub or scrape is sufficient. Whether older carrots are peeled or scrubbed is a matter of taste. Small carrots are best cooked whole by boiling or steaming briefly. Medium and large carrots may be halved, quartered, cut in sticks or sliced. Boil, steam or stir fry them. To glaze carrots, cut them into fine strips and cook them in a little water with a knob of butter. By the time the carrots are just tender the water should have evaporated, leaving the vegetables coated in a glossy glaze. A little sugar may be added when cooking old carrots. The carrots should be stirred or the pan shaken often to prevent them burning.

Small new carrots take about 5-7 minutes to boil until tender; older carrots take 10-15 minutes, depending on size. Carrots may be cooked for slightly longer, then mashed with swede or potatoes. Well cooked carrots may also be rubbed through a sieve or puréed in a food processor, then enriched with a little butter and cream.

Carrots are an essential flavouring vegetable for soups, stocks and stews. They are also valuable in mince dishes and they make delicious soup. Grated carrot is a useful salad ingredient and this versatile vegetable may also be used in preserves and sweet dishes, such as carrot cake or a lightly spiced Indian dessert. Carrot marmalade was a clever war-time invention as a substitute for orange preserve: the finely cut carrots were flavoured with orange rind and juice and cooked in syrup.

CAULIFLOWER

Green and purple cauliflowers are now available in addition to the more familiar white-headed vegetables, and very small cauliflowers are cultivated as individual portions. Look for firm, white unblemished vegetables that are neatly packed with a small amount of green leaves. Avoid soft, rubbery cauliflowers or any that have very long stalks and loose heads. Cauliflowers that are not perfectly white are not necessarily inferior in flavour, provided that they are good quality in other respects. It is as well, however, to avoid any that have softening brown patches or have been trimmed.

Cauliflowers may be cooked whole or divided into florets. Boiling, steaming or stir frying are the most common cooking methods. Used raw or

25

briefly blanched, cauliflower florets make very good additions to salads, and they may be coated in cheese-flavoured choux pastry, then deep fried to make delicious savoury fritters.

Overcooked cauliflower is soft, watery and tasteless. About 5-7 minutes is sufficient boiling time for florets and a whole cauliflower should not be boiled for more than 10-15 minutes. Steaming is a particularly good cooking method for cauliflower. For florets allow the same time as for boiling; when steaming a whole cauliflower increase the cooking time to 20-30 minutes, depending on the size of the vegetable.

Serve cauliflower plain, with a little butter; coated with a cheese sauce; or topped with fried breadcrumbs. Cauliflower is excellent in vegetable curry, it makes good soup (particularly topped with cheese) or it may be puréed and enriched with cream or fromage frais.

CELERIAC

This is a cream-coloured root vegetable, about the same size as a swede and with a similarly thick skin. It has a delicate flavour reminiscent of celery. To prepare celeriac, peel and trim it, then plunge it straight into a bowl of acidulated water as it discolours quickly.

Cut celeriac into neat cubes or sticks and cook in a saucepan of boiling water until tender, about 8-10 minutes for small pieces. If preferred, the vegetable may be cut into large chunks and boiled for 15-20 minutes, then mashed with butter and pepper. Boiling is a better option than steaming, although finely cut celeriac may be steamed in packets of mixed vegetables or as a flavouring for fish and poultry.

Celeriac may also be served raw, usually coarsely grated or finely shredded. If adding it to long-cooked soups and stews, put it in towards the end of the cooking time or it may become very soft. It also makes good soup. Plain cooked celeriac (in chunks or slices) is delicious coated with cheese sauce.

CELERY

A versatile vegetable for serving raw or cooked, or using as a flavouring ingredient. Look for firm, unblemished heads of celery with leaves that are bright and crisp. Stalks with large ribs may be stringy. Trimmed celery hearts are also available for braising whole. Canned celery hearts are a useful storecupboard standby for wrapping in cooked ham and coating in cheese sauce as a supper dish.

The top of the head and stalk ends should be cut off but not discarded. The leaves and stalk tops may be used as part of a bouquet garni or they may be reserved for garnish. Cut up small, they are perfectly good in salads, soups and stews, as are the chopped stalks.

Remove stalks from the celery as required, scrub them well and cut off any blemished parts. Slice the celery or cut it into lengths for cooking. If a recipe calls for diced or chopped celery, cut the stalks into thin strips lengthways before slicing them across into small pieces. Cut into very thin strips, about

5 cm / 2 inches long, then soaked for about 30 minutes in iced water, celery is excellent in salads.

Serve lengths of raw celery with dips or cheese. Braise lengths or hearts with a small amount of sautéed onion and diced carrot in a little stock or wine. Cook for about 40-60 minutes, depending on size and age, until the celery is tender. The cooking juices may be thickened with beurre manié to serve as an accompanying sauce.

Stir frying is a good cooking method for celery. The sticks should be sliced thinly or cut into fine strips. Slicing at an angle is an Oriental technique popular for stir fries. Celery may also be cooked by boiling and steaming. Boil for 10-20 minutes, depending on size and age; or steam for up to 30 minutes.

CHICORY
Small oval heads of pale, closely packed leaves tipped with yellow, chicory has a slightly bitter flavour. It may be used raw in salads or braised until tender. The American name for chicory is endive.

Trim off the stalk end of each head and wash well. Cut the head across into slices for mixing into salads or separate the leaves and use them as a base for serving a variety of dishes. The whole leaves may also be served with dips.

Chicory may be boiled in a saucepan of acidulated water until tender – about 15-20 minutes – but the preferred cooking method is braising. Cook a small amount of finely chopped onion in butter or oil, then turn the chicory heads in the fat. Pour in stock or wine to come about a third to halfway up the heads. Cover and braise for 30-60 minutes depending on the size of the chicory heads, until tender throughout. Turn once or twice. The cooking juices may be thickened and poured over the chicory heads.

CHINESE LEAVES
Also known as Chinese cabbage. A tall, fairly loosely packed vegetable consisting mainly of tender crunchy stalks edged by pale green-yellow leaves. The vegetable has a mild, cabbage-like flavour. It may be shredded for use in salads or stir fries. Thicker slices may be added to sauced dishes, usually well-seasoned Chinese braised mixtures, and cooked very briefly. Overcooking gives limp, tasteless results.

COURGETTES
Both green and yellow varieties are available. Look for firm, unblemished vegetables. Trim off the ends and peel the courgettes if liked, although they may be cooked with the peel on. Cut courgettes into slices, chunks or sticks, or grate them. They may be halved and baked with a topping, or their centres scooped out and a stuffing added.

Basic cooking methods include steaming, braising, baking, sautéing, stir frying and shallow frying. Although courgettes may be boiled, this cooking method does not do them justice as even brief boiling tends to oversoften the delicate flesh. Coated in batter or breadcrumbs, courgettes are also delicious

27

deep fried. In Italy and America, where the vegetable is known as zucchini, the flowers are regarded as a delicacy and are frequently coated in light batter and deep fried.

For steaming, wrap sliced courgettes in foil; cook for about 10 minutes. Sautéing and stir frying are excellent methods. Thinly cut vegetables will require 2–5 minutes. Baking is a practical method when the courgettes are served with a baked dish; simply dot them with butter, sprinkle them with salt and pepper and cook in a covered dish for 15-30 minutes at 180°C / 350°F / gas 4. Braise courgettes with onions and tomatoes or other vegetables, allowing about 20 minutes' cooking, or up to 45 minutes depending on the way in which the vegetables are cut and the other ingredients.

CUCUMBER

Although they are usually eaten raw in salads, cucumbers are also good braised. Buy firm, bright green medium-sized cucumbers. Avoid any with very dark, thick-looking skins, as these may have large seeds, poor texture and an unacceptably strong flavour.

Cucumbers may be peeled, partially peeled or served with the peel on for salads. The classic preparation is to slice the cucumber very thinly, sprinkle it with a little salt and allow it to drain in a colander for 10 minutes before use. This extracts the excess liquid from the vegetable. Having been prepared in this way, the cucumber slices may be dried on absorbent kitchen paper and used to make delicious sandwiches. They may also be topped with a little chopped mint or snipped chives for serving as a plain salad. An oil and vinegar dressing, or cider vinegar, are classic additions.

Grated or diced cucumber may be mixed with plain yogurt to make a dip or side dish for spicy food. Add garlic and a little chopped onion to make tzatziki, a Greek starter served with plenty of crusty bread.

Peel cucumber before cooking, then cut it into 5 cm / 2 inch lengths. The seeds are usually scooped out. Braise trimmed cucumber in stock for about 20 minutes. Dill or mint may be added before serving and the sauce may be enriched with soured cream. Sticks of cucumber may be stir fried briefly.

ENDIVE

This resembles a curly lettuce. It has firm leaves which are usually pale yellow-green with darker green tips. To prepare endive, trim off the stalk, wash well and use in salads. The American term for endive is chicory.

FENNEL

Florence fennel is a bulbous vegetable with a texture like that of celery and an aniseed flavour. There are usually a few fronds of feathery leaves attached to the trimmed stalks at the top of the bulbs – these may be reserved for garnishing or used in cooking.

Trim away tough stalk ends, then thoroughly wash and slice fennel for use in salads. Fennel discolours easily when cut, so always use a stainless steel knife and use the vegetable as soon as possible after cutting. The bulbs may be braised as for celery, either whole or as halves and cook in about 1-1¼ hours.

KOHLRABI

This is the swollen stem of a member of the cabbage family, sold trimmed of stems and leaves. It has a flavour slightly similar to swede. Either purple or green skinned, and ranging in size from that of a large potato to a small swede, kohlrabi may be served raw or cooked.

Peel the vegetable and place it in a bowl of acidulated water. For serving raw, kohlrabi should be grated or cut into small pieces. Small kohlrabi may be boiled whole; larger vegetables should be sliced or cut into chunks. Cook in boiling water for 15-45 minutes or until tender. Follow the longer time if cooking whole vegetables.

Sticks of kohlrabi may be stir fried with other vegetables, such as leeks or onions. Diced or cubed kohlrabi may be added to soups, stews or casseroles.

LEEKS

These vary considerably in size. Look for firm, well-formed vegetables with a good ratio of white to green. Trim off the ends and slice, then wash in a colander, separating the slices into rings. Alternatively, slit the leeks three-quarters through down their length, then open each one out and hold it under cold running water to wash away all the grit.

Leeks may be boiled, steamed, fried, stewed, braised or baked. Allow 10-20 minutes for boiling or steaming, selecting the longer time for large lengths or small whole vegetables. Drain well and serve coated with cheese sauce. Alternatively, top with grated cheese and breadcrumbs and grill until brown. Fry sliced leeks in butter until tender but not soft – about 15 minutes – or stir fry them with other vegetables. Add leeks to soups and stews or use them to flavour stocks.

LETTUCE

There is a wide variety of lettuces on offer all year. These are the most common types:

Round The traditional British salad leaf; a loosely packed bright vegetable with a small heart. Flavour and texture are not particularly interesting.

Cos Lettuce A tall, dark-leafed lettuce with crisp firm leaves and a good flavour.

Webb's Wonderful A round lettuce with slightly wrinkled, crisp dark leaves, and a firm heart.

Iceberg Tightly packed, pale green lettuce with very crisp leaves and a good flavour.

Lamb's Lettuce Small oval-leafed plants, resembling immature round lettuce but darker.

Lollo Rosso / Lollo Biondo A frilly, firm-textured lettuce which is loosely packed. The lollo rosso variety has dark leaves fringed with deep red, whereas the *biondo* type has pale-edged leaves.

Wash all lettuce well and discard any tough or damaged stalks. It is traditional to tear lettuce by hand rather than to shred it with a knife, but this is a matter for personal taste. Never prepare lettuce a long time before serving.

Although lettuce is usually served raw, it is also delicious when braised with a little finely chopped onion in stock or wine. Fresh peas braised with lettuce is a classic French dish. Allow about 30 minutes' gentle cooking in a small amount of liquid and use a covered pan or dish.

MARROW

From the same family as courgettes and pumpkin, marrow has a tough skin and soft, fibrous centre with lots of seeds surrounded by firm flesh. Cut the vegetable in half or slice it into rings, then remove the soft flesh and seeds before peeling thickly.

Marrow may be baked, braised, steamed, stir fried or boiled, the latter being the least interesting cooking method. Overcooked marrow is watery and mushy, particularly when boiled. Baking or braising with onions and herbs are the best methods. Chunks of marrow (about 5 cm / 2 inches in size) take about 40 minutes to bake at 180°C / 350°F / gas 4, depending on the other ingredients added. They may also be braised for about 30 minutes with onions and herbs, either in their own juice or with tomatoes or a little wine or cider.

Stuffings for marrow range from meat mixtures to rice or breadcrumb fillings. Rings or halves may be stuffed, or the vegetable may be laid on its side and a thick slice removed from the top as a lid. The hollowed-out marrow may then be stuffed and the 'lid' replaced. Bake the stuffed marrow until tender, then remove the 'lid' to allow the stuffing to brown. At 180°C / 350°F / gas 4, a medium-sized whole marrow will require 1¼–1¾ hours to bake, whereas rings cook in 45 minutes-1¼ hours, depending on size and filling.

Marrow may also be used as a key ingredient for making chutney. It is usually combined with fruit, such as apples, and lots of onions for flavour. It may also be cooked with ginger and used to add bulk to jam.

MUSHROOMS

Most of the mushrooms available in greengrocers and supermarkets are the same variety, differing only in the stage of development at which they have been harvested. Fully open or flat mushrooms traditionally known as field mushrooms are the most mature. They may be recognized by their dark gills and large heads. Flat mushrooms have good flavour but tend to discolour dishes to which they are added, so are usually used for grilling and stuffing.

Wild mushrooms are a separate issue from cultivated varieties. Before they are gathered, a specialist source of information should be consulted to avoid any danger of consuming a poisonous species. Some specialist stores sell wild mushrooms but they are most commonly available dried from delicatessens.

Cultivated mushrooms do not require peeling. Trim tough stalks from shiitake or oyster mushrooms. Rinse mushrooms, gills down under slowly running cold water, rubbing them gently. Alternatively, simply wipe them with dampened absorbent kitchen paper. Never leave mushrooms to soak as they will absorb water, ruining both texture and flavour.

Mushrooms may be brushed with a little fat and grilled, flat or on skewers. They may also be poached in a little milk, stock or wine for a few minutes. Alternatively, whole or cut-up mushrooms may be shallow fried or stir fried in oil or butter, either whole or cut up. Coated with egg and breadcrumbs, dipped in choux pastry or batter, button mushrooms are delicious deep fried. They are also excellent baked, particularly when topped with breadcrumbs and cheese.

For frying or poaching, allow about 5-15 minutes' cooking time. Allow 15-30 minutes for baking, depending on the topping or stuffing. Grill mushrooms briefly for about 5 minutes, gills uppermost.

Pale mushrooms may be added to sauces and soups; all types are suitable for flavouring stews, the choice depending on the colour of the stew.

Cup mushrooms or open mushrooms are pale in colour and have a lip around the edge. They are useful for stuffing.

Button mushrooms may be fully closed or partially closed, with little of the gill area showing. They vary in size; very small buttons are perfect for adding whole to casseroles and sauces. Button mushrooms are ideal for sauces and pale dishes which require a delicate colour and flavour.

31

In addition to the grades of cultivated mushroom described above, at least three other types of fresh mushroom are commonly available:

Chestnut mushrooms have a darker skin than ordinary mushrooms and a more pronounced flavour. They are usually sold as large buttons.

Oyster mushrooms are flat and pale creamy-yellow in colour with a soft texture and delicate flavour. They break easily and require very little cooking.

Shiitake are strongly flavoured mushrooms from China and Japan. They are popular in Oriental cooking. They are usually sold dried in delicatessens and Oriental supermarkets, when their flavour is very pronounced, but are also available fresh. The fresh mushrooms are darker than cultivated British field mushrooms and they tend to have a firmer, slightly more rubbery texture.

OKRA

Also known as ladies' fingers, these pale green ridged pods vary in size, the smaller ones being the most tender. Look for unblemished whole vegetables with the stalks intact. Trim off the stalk ends and wash well. The okra pods may be cooked whole or sliced before cooking. Do not prepare the vegetable too far in advance of cooking as slices may discolour.

Okra contains a gum-like substance that seeps out of the pods during long cooking to thicken stews and braised dishes. Typical dishes with okra include *gumbo*, a classic Creole stew, and spiced okra with onions, which is often served as a side dish in Indian restaurants. Okra may also be stuffed and braised or baked.

Cooking times for okra should either be brief, using fierce heat, or long enough to tenderize the pods. Sliced okra may be coated in flour and seasonings or spices, then shallow or deep fried for a few minutes until browned. Slices may also be braised briefly or added to casseroles and stews towards the end of cooking; however, the vegetable quickly becomes slimy when sliced and long-cooked by moist methods. Whole pods may be braised with onions, tomatoes and garlic until tender – about 15-30 minutes, depending on the size and age of the pods.

ONIONS

Large Spanish onions are the mildest variety. These are ideal for boiling whole and serving with butter or a sauce, or for stuffing. The medium-sized common onions, most often used in cooking, are stronger in flavour. Small, pickling or button onions have a strong flavour. They may be boiled and coated with sauce or peeled and added whole to casseroles. Cocktail, or silverskin, onions are tiny. They are sometimes available fresh but are most often sold pickled in vinegar. Spring- or salad onions have not formed bulbs. They have a dense white base leading to hollow green ends. Once trimmed, the whole of the onion may be used raw or in cooking. Shallots and Welsh onions are small onions. Each shallot consists of two or three cloves, similar in shape to garlic cloves, clumped together inside the papery skin. They are mild in flavour and may be peeled and chopped or used whole. The tops from fresh young shallots may also be used in cooking, rather like chives.

Onions are often fried briefly as a preliminary cooking stage in more complicated dishes. The aim is to soften the onion but not brown it, and the cooking process will only be completed when the onion has been incorporated with other ingredients and cooked until tender. Browning onions by frying requires significantly longer cooking, depending on the number cooked. Onions shrink significantly when fried until brown, and this should be done over moderate heat, turning occasionally, for about 20-30 minutes until the onions are golden and evenly cooked. If fried by this method they will be tender and flavoursome. Onions that are browned quickly over too high a heat will not be cooked through, but simply scorched outside.

Onions may also be boiled or steamed. Allow 30 minutes for small onions or up to 1¼ hours for large ones. Large onions may be baked whole, washed but unpeeled, until very tender, then split and filled or topped with butter.

PARSNIPS

Look for firm, unblemished parsnips. To prepare them, peel, then cut them in half, in chunks or slices. They may be boiled, steamed or roasted.

Chunks of parsnip will be tender when boiled for 10 minutes; larger pieces require about 20 minutes. When tender, drain well and serve with a soured cream sauce, or mash with butter and pepper.

To roast parsnips arrange them around a joint of meat or in a separate dish and brush with fat. Allow about 45 minutes-1¼ hours at 180-190°C / 350-375°F / gas 4-5, until tender and golden.

Parsnips are delicious in mixed vegetable curry and may also be added to soups and stews. Parsnip fritters may be made by coating par-boiled vegetables in batter and deep frying them until golden.

PEAS

Fresh peas are in season from May to September. Look for bright, fresh plump pods. The peas inside should be neither bullet-hard nor very large as they can become very dry in texture and particularly dull in flavour. Allow about 350-400 g / 12-14 oz per person as a good deal of weight is lost to the pods.

Split the pods over a colander and slide the peas out using a fingertip. Wash well, then add to a small amount of just boiling water. Cook for 7-10 minutes, until the peas are tender. Alternatively, peas may be steamed for 15-20 minutes. It is traditional to add a sprig of mint to the water when cooking peas which are to be served with lamb.

Mange Tout The name means 'eat all', a fitting description. Mange tout are flat pea pods with tiny peas just forming inside. The entire pod is edible, excluding the stalk, which is trimmed. Mange tout may be cooked in boiling water for 2-3 minutes, or steamed for up to 5 minutes, but are at their best when stir fried for 3-5 minutes.

Sugar Snaps These are small peas enclosed in edible pods. They have an excellent flavour. Everything is edible except the stalk, which should be trimmed. Cook sugar snaps in a saucepan of boiling water for 3-5 minutes, or by steaming for about 5 minutes. They are a more substantial and flavoursome vegetable than mange tout.

PEPPERS

Large sweet or bell peppers come from the capsicum family. They are also known as pimento (or pimientos when bottled). The most common type is the green pepper, which changes colour as it ripens, first to yellow and then to red. A variety of other colours is also available, including white and purple-black.

To prepare a pepper, remove the stalk end and cut out the core from the inside. Discard the ribs, pith and seeds. The pepper shell may then be rinsed free of seeds and drained.

Peppers are used in a variety of ways: they may be eaten raw in salads or crudités; lightly cooked in stir fries; stuffed and baked or braised; grilled on skewers; or stewed slowly with meat, poultry or other vegetables.

When raw they have a crunchy texture and fresh flavour, but when cooked they soften and their flavour mellows. Some salad recipes require peppers to be charred, then skinned.

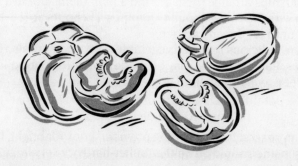

POTATOES

These may be loosely divided into new and old, the former being the thin-skinned, spring crop for immediate consumption and the latter being the second crop of thicker-skinned potatoes grown for winter storage. The choice is always changing, with imported varieties and new strains constantly being developed.

Avoid buying or eating potatoes that have turned green. Cut out any eyes and sprouting areas from potatoes in preparation. Store potatoes in a cool, dry place in thick brown paper bags that exclude all light.

Although new potatoes are now available all year, Jerseys are the traditional 'first' new potatoes in the shops. Imported early in the year, from Christmas or even before, these have a fine flavour but are expensive. Small, waxy and firm, they are ideal for steaming or boiling. Small, waxy 'salad' potatoes are also available all year at a price.

The following are good all round, old potatoes for boiling, mashing, baking and frying: King Edward, Redskin, Maris Piper, Pentland Hawk, Pentland Ivory and Desirée. Majestic tend to break up easily when boiled, so they are better for baking and frying. Pentland Squire are floury and good for baking, as are Cara, because they are large and even in size and shape.

Boiling Peel the potatoes, if liked, or scrub them well. Remove all eyes and blemishes and any green areas. Cut large potatoes in half or into quarters and place in a saucepan. Cover with cold water, add salt if wished, and bring to the boil. Reduce the heat, partly cover the pan and cook for about 20 minutes. Small chunks cook in about 10-15 minutes (useful for mashing); larger, unpeeled, potatoes take somewhat longer. New potatoes cook more quickly, in 10-15 minutes.

Baking An easy cooking method, this is discussed, with serving suggestions, on page 90. Floury potatoes – the sort that do not boil well – give best results for baking. Scrub the potatoes well and prick them all over to prevent them from bursting. Potatoes may be brushed with oil if wished.

Roasting Peeled potatoes, cut in halves or quarters, may either be roasted from raw or parboiled for 5-10 minutes, dusted with plain flour, and then added to the hot fat in the roasting tin. They should be coated in hot fat and turned once or twice during cooking. For crisp results, raw potatoes will take 1-1½ hours, depending on the size of the potatoes and the oven temperature. Parboiled potatoes require about 1 hour at 190°C/375°F/gas 5.

Chipped Potatoes Cut the thoroughly scrubbed, or washed and peeled, potatoes into thick fingers, dry with absorbent kitchen paper and deep fry in oil at 190°C/375°F until just beginning to brown. Lift the chips out of the oil and drain them well. Bring the oil back to the original cooking temperature. Lower the chips into the oil again and cook for a couple of minutes more, until crisp and golden. Drain well on absorbent kitchen paper and serve at once.

PUMPKIN
Pumpkin belongs to the same family as marrow. Pumpkins vary enormously in size. Small ones may be sold whole, but you are more likely to encounter wedges cut from a large vegetable.

The central soft core of seeds should be removed and the orange-coloured flesh thickly peeled. The flesh is firmer than that of marrow and is delicious roasted, baked or braised with onions, herbs and bacon and a cheese topping for about an hour. Pumpkin may also be boiled and mashed or steamed for 30-45 minutes and puréed for use in savoury and sweet dishes, particularly the American sweet and spicy pumpkin pie. Pumpkin also makes good soup.

RADISHES
These are usually eaten raw in salads or as crudités; however, large white radishes are also combined with other ingredients in stir fries and steamed Oriental-style dishes.

Small round red radishes are the most common, but the long white radish known as *mooli* or *daikon* (in Japanese cooking) is becoming increasingly popular. Red radishes require no preparation other than washing, topping and tailing. Large white radishes must be peeled. Very large, old white radishes can be fibrous, stringy and unpleasant even when cut finely.

SALSIFY AND SCORZONERA
These root vegetables are in season from October to May. Salsify is a creamy colour and scorzonera is black. Although both have a delicate flavour, scorzonera is considered to be salsify's superior.

Do not use a carbon steel knife to prepare these vegetables and cook them as soon as possible after preparation, or they may discolour. The moment the vegetables have been trimmed and peeled, put them into acidulated water. To cook, cut into lengths or fingers and add to a saucepan of salted boiling water to which a little lemon juice has been added. Cook for 20-30 minutes, or until tender. Drain and serve with butter or with a coating sauce such as Béchamel or Hollandaise.

Salsify or scorzonera which has been three-quarters cooked by boiling may be drained and fried in butter before serving or coated in a light batter and deep fried to make fritters.

SEAKALE
Resembling celery stalks surrounded by dark green, tough, frilly leaves, seakale grows wild on the beaches of South East England between December and May and is also found in Western Europe. Although it is also cultivated, it is seldom available in the shops. Cultivated seakale is blanched during growth to give long tender stalks which are boiled until tender. The young leaves of the cultivated plant may also be eaten. To prepare wild seakale, wash it thoroughly and trim off the thick, tough stalk. It should be freshly cooked in a small amount of boiling water for about 15 minutes, or until tender, then thoroughly drained and used like spinach.

SORREL
Sorrel is used both as a vegetable and a herb. There are many varieties, some quite bitter. It should be treated as spinach, with a little sugar added to taste during cooking to counteract the natural acidity.

SPINACH
There are winter and summer varieties of this versatile, easy-to-cook vegetable. Since it shrinks considerably on cooking, allow about 225 g / 8 oz fresh spinach per portion.

Wash the leaves well and trim off any tough stalk ends. Pack the wet leaves into a large saucepan and cover with a tight-fitting lid. Place over moderate to high heat and cook for about 3 minutes, shaking the pan often, until the spinach has wilted. Lower the heat slightly, if necessary, and cook for 3-5 minutes more, or until the spinach is tender. Drain well in a sieve, squeezing out all the liquid if the vegetable is to be chopped.

Serve spinach tossed with butter and pepper or a little nutmeg. It may be used in a variety of pasta dishes, pies, quiches, soufflés and soups. Spinach is delicious with scrambled or poached eggs, poached fish or grilled chicken.

SQUASH
Squash is an American term applied to marrow and a wide variety of vegetables of the same family. Availability in Britain and Europe is somewhat unpredictable; however these are a few of the main types:

Butternut Squash A small vegetable with pale, beige-peach coloured skin and deep orange-coloured flesh. The halved vegetable has a small central hollow for seeds, so that it resembles a large avocado. The whole or halved squash is usually baked or roasted.

Crookneck This is a large, rough-skinned, long-bodied yellow squash. As its name suggests it has a long narrow, curved neck. Treat as for marrow.

Custard Marrow A pale, flat, fluted squash.

Hubbard Squash A melon-shaped gourd with rough green skin, this may be treated as marrow once peeled.

Spaghetti Squash Oval, yellow-skinned squash about the size of a large yellow melon. It gets its name from the flesh, which resembles spaghetti when cooked. The squash should be boiled or steamed whole, or halved and wrapped in foil, for 20-50 minutes, depending on size. When cooked, halve the squash if necessary, discard the seeds from the middle and use a fork to scoop out the strands of flesh. These are at their best when still slightly crunchy. They have plenty of flavour and are delicious topped with butter and cheese or any sauce suitable for pasta.

SWEDES

Large, inexpensive root vegetables with thick skin and pale orange flesh. Wash, trim and peel thickly, then cut into chunks for cooking. Boil for 20-30 minutes, or until tender, then drain thoroughly and mash with butter and pepper. This is the traditional accompaniment for haggis. Swedes may also be mashed with carrots or potatoes.

The diced vegetable is excellent in soups and stews. Puréed cooked swede may be used in soufflé mixtures.

SWEETCORN

Corn cobs are surrounded by silky threads and an outer covering of leafy husks, which must be removed before cooking unless the corn is to be cooked on a barbecue. The kernels are pale when raw, becoming more strongly yellow in colour on cooking.

Place the corn cobs in a pan with water to cover and bring to the boil. Do not add salt as this toughens the kernels. Simmer for about 10 minutes, or until the corn kernels are tender and come away easily from the cob. Drain well and serve topped with a little butter. Corn holders – pronged utensils inserted at either end of the cob – make it possible to eat these tasty vegetables without burning your fingers. For using in salads or other dishes, the cooked kernels may be scraped off the cobs using a kitchen knife. It is usually simpler, however, to use frozen or canned sweetcorn kernels, both of which are of excellent quality.

Whole cobs may be baked in their husks or barbecued. Carefully fold back the husks and remove the silky threads, then wash well and drain. Fold the husks back over the corn. Cook over medium coals or roast in the oven at 190°C/375°F/gas 5 for about 40 minutes, or until the kernels are tender.

SWEET POTATOES

In spite of their name, these are not potatoes at all, but are red-skinned, large vegetables with pale orange flesh and a slightly sweet flavour. Sweet potatoes may be baked or boiled in their skins. To boil, allow about 30-40 minutes, depending on size. Bake as for ordinary potatoes. Once cooked, peel and cut into cubes, then toss with butter and a little nutmeg. Alternatively, mash with butter and nutmeg or a little mace.

Sweet potatoes are used in a variety of sweet and savoury dishes.

SWISS CHARD
The leaves of this vegetable may be cooked exactly as for spinach, giving very similar results. The tender stalks, which resemble thin, wide celery sticks, are delicious when lightly cooked in boiling water and served with butter. Allow about 5 minutes to cook tender stalks. Serve them as a separate vegetable or starter, perhaps with Hollandaise or with some grated Parmesan cheese.

TOMATOES
Although tomatoes are technically fruit, they are used as a vegetable. Of the many varieties available, all may be used raw and many are ideal for cooking. Freshly picked sun-ripened tomatoes are delicious, but it is worth investigating some of the other varieties.

Cherry Tomatoes Very small tomatoes, these can have an excellent sweet flavour when ripe. However, some purchased tomatoes can be sharp and lacking in flavour. These are ideal for salads or for skewering with other ingredients for kebabs.

Marmande, Beef or Beefsteak Tomatoes Very large tomatoes that are ideal for stuffing. They should be a good deep red when ripe. Sun-ripened large tomatoes have an outstanding flavour. Sadly this is seldom found in purchased fruit, which is usually picked well before it is ripe.

Plum Tomatoes Deep red, oval, small to medium-sized fruit. Plum tomatoes have a good flavour and are valued for cooking and as the prime ingredient in tomato purée. They are also good in salads.

Yellow Tomatoes Large or cherry-sized, these tomatoes are sweet when ripe but can lack flavour when picked too early. They should be a rich yellow colour. Used mainly raw, yellow tomatoes may be cooked with yellow peppers, yellow courgettes and white aubergines in a pale version of ratatouille.

Cooking methods for tomatoes include grilling and frying. They are usually cut in half – or in slices for speed – and are traditionally served with grilled meat or fish, mixed grill or as part of a traditional cooked breakfast. Grilled or fried tomatoes on toast make a good snack or light meal. Baked tomatoes are usually scooped out and filled with a rice- or breadcrumb-based stuffing or a minced meat mixture.

TURNIPS

Small, round summer turnips have delicate flavour. They are ideal for cooking whole and serving as a vegetable accompaniment. Larger main crop turnips are better suited to dicing or cutting into chunks and using in soups and stews or casseroles.

To prepare turnips, trim off the ends and remove the peel; small young vegetables need only be peeled thinly. Cook small whole turnips in a saucepan of boiling acidulated water for about 15 minutes, or until tender. Drain well and toss with butter and parsley or serve generously coated with cheese, Béchamel or Hollandaise sauce.

Larger turnips may be boiled, drained and mashed or puréed. Matchstick sticks of turnip are suitable for stir frying or baking in foil with parsnips and carrots cut to a similar size. Small, young turnips may also be parboiled, then glazed with the minimum of liquid and a little butter as for carrots.

The leaves of fresh young turnips may be trimmed from their stalks and cooked as for cabbage.

YAMS

These tubers resemble large potatoes, with white, floury flesh. Scrub and boil yams in their skin.

There are a number of vegetables available which belong to the yam and cassava family, including small dark and hairy eddoes. These vegetables must not be eaten raw as they contain natural toxins: in fact, prepared cassava should be soaked in water for about 30 minutes before cooking.

Note More information and methods of cooking, including microwave instructions are listed, where appropriate, under individual recipes and in the feature on microwave cooking on page 114.

SOUPS

Fish Stock

fish bones and trimmings
  without gills, which cause
  bitterness
5 ml / 1 tsp salt
1 small onion, sliced
2 celery sticks, sliced
4 white peppercorns
1 bouquet garni

Break up any bones and wash the fish trimmings, if used. Put the bones, trimmings or heads in a saucepan and cover with 1 litre / 1¾ pints cold water. Add the salt.

Bring the liquid to the boil and add the vegetables, peppercorns and bouquet garni. Lower the heat, cover and simmer gently for 30-40 minutes. Do not cook the stock for longer than 40 minutes or it may develop a bitter taste. Strain, cool quickly and use as required.

MAKES ABOUT 1 LITRE / 1¾ PINTS

VARIATION

White Wine Fish Stock Add 100 ml / 3½ fl oz dry white wine, 4-5 mushroom stalks and 1 sliced carrot. Simmer for 30 minutes only.

NUTRITION NOTE

Food values are not included for the stock recipes and consommé as they do not contain significant quantities of these nutrients.

Rich Strong Stock

This recipe makes a large quantity of stock which freezes well for future use. Although the quantities may be reduced, a large volume of liquid is required to cover marrow bones. It is more practical to invest in a large stockpot or saucepan and to boil a large quantity occasionally than to reduce the weight of ingredients in proportion to water to make a weaker meat stock.

675 g / 1½ lb shin of beef on the bone
675 g / 1½ lb knuckle of veal on the bone, or other stewing veal
450 g / 1 lb beef marrow bones
1 chicken drumstick or poultry trimmings
1 onion, sliced
1 carrot, quartered
100 g / 4 oz gammon or bacon, diced
1 small turnip, roughly chopped
2 celery sticks, quartered
2 open cup mushrooms, quartered
1 tomato, quartered
1 bouquet garni
4 white peppercorns
2 cloves
1 blade of mace

Set the oven at 200°C / 400°F / gas 6. Put the bones in a roasting tin and roast for about 2 hours until browned.

Transfer the bones to a large saucepan. Pour off the fat from the tin, add some boiling water and stir to scrape all the sediment off the tin. Then add to the bones in the pan. Add the onion and carrot.

Add about 5.6 litres / 10 pints water to cover the bones generously. Bring to the boil, skim the surface, then lower the heat and add the remaining ingredients. Simmer for about 5 hours. Cool, then strain. Skim off surface fat. Season and use as required.

MAKES ABOUT 5.3 LITRES / 9 PINTS

Chicken Stock

4 chicken drumsticks or
  1 meaty chicken carcass
1 small onion, sliced
1 carrot, roughly chopped
1 celery stick, sliced
1 bouquet garni
5 ml / 1 tsp white
  peppercorns

Break or chop the carcass into manageable pieces. Put the drumsticks or carcass in a large saucepan with 1.75 litres / 3 pints cold water. Bring to the boil, then skim any scum off the surface.

Add the remaining ingredients, lower the heat and simmer for 3-4 hours. Cool quickly, then strain. Skim off surface fat. Season and use as required.

MAKES ABOUT 1.4 LITRES / 2½ PINTS

VARIATIONS

Rich Chicken Stock Use drumsticks and roast them at 200°C / 400°F / gas 6 for 40 minutes. Drain off the fat. Continue as above, adding 225 g / 8 oz cubed belly pork with the chicken.
Game Stock Use the carcasses of 1 or 2 game birds such as pheasant or grouse, with the giblets, instead of the chicken.

Vegetable Stock

Vary the vegetables according to the market selection
and your personal taste.

2 onions, sliced
2 leeks, trimmed, sliced and
  washed
1 small turnip, chopped
4 celery sticks, sliced
2 tomatoes, chopped
1 bouquet garni
6 black peppercorns
2 cloves
a few lettuce, spinach and
  watercress leaves
2.5 ml / ½ tsp yeast extract
  (optional)
salt

Put the root vegetables, celery, tomatoes, herbs and spices in a large saucepan. Add 2 litres / 3½ pints water. Bring to the boil, lower the heat and simmer for 1 hour.

Add the lettuce, spinach and watercress and simmer for 1 hour more. Stir in the yeast extract, if using, and add salt to taste. Strain and use as required.

MAKES ABOUT 1.75 LITRES / 3 PINTS

Consommé

100 g / 4 oz lean shin of beef, trimmed of all fat, finely shredded
1 small onion, sliced
1 small carrot, sliced
1 small celery stick, sliced
1.25 litres / 2¼ pints cold Rich Strong Stock (page 43)
1 bouquet garni
1.25 ml / ¼ tsp salt
4 white peppercorns
white and crushed shell of 1 egg

Before you begin, scald a large enamel or stainless steel (not aluminium) saucepan, a piece of clean muslin or thin white cotton, a metal sieve and a whisk in boiling water. Put the meat in a large bowl, add 125 ml / 4 fl oz water and set aside to soak for 15 minutes.

Transfer the meat and soaking liquid to the pan. Add the vegetables, stock, bouquet garni, salt and peppercorns. Finally add the egg white and shell. Heat slowly to simmering point, whisking constantly. A thick white crust of foam will develop on the top.

Remove the whisk, cover the pan and simmer the stock very gently for 1-2 hours. Do not allow the stock to boil or the froth will break up and cloud the consommé.

Line the sieve with the muslin and place it over a perfectly clean bowl. Strain the crust and liquid very gently through the muslin into the bowl. Try not to break the crust. The consommé should be sparkling clear.

Transfer to a clean saucepan, reheat and add more salt and pepper if required.

SERVES 4

VARIATIONS

Consommé Madrilene Add 450 g / 1 lb chopped fresh or canned tomatoes and 1 sliced green pepper to the vegetables when making the consommé. Substitute 1 litre / 1¾ pints Chicken Stock (page 44) for the Rich Strong Stock and simmer very gently for 1 hour. Serve hot or iced, with a garnish of 2 peeled and diced tomatoes.

Prawn and Tomato Soup

FOOD VALUES	TOTAL	PER PORTION
Protein	355g	89g
Carbohydrate	1130g	283g
Fat	94g	24g
Fibre	54g	14g
kcals	6495	1624

450 g / 1 lb whole cooked
  prawns
150 ml / ¼ pint cider
  vinegar
1 blade of mace
900 g / 2 lb tomatoes
1 crisp breakfast roll, made
  into crumbs
1.1 litres / 2 pints Fish Stock
  (page 42)
50 g / 2 oz vermicelli, broken
  into short pieces
15 ml / 1 tbsp anchovy
  essence or mushroom
  ketchup
salt and pepper

Peel the prawns, placing the shells in a saucepan and reserving the flesh. Add the cider vinegar to the shells with 150 ml / ¼ pint water, the blade of mace the the tomatoes. Bring to the boil, reduce the heat and cover the pan. Simmer for 30 minutes, until the tomatoes are reduced to a pulp. Strain the mixture through a fine sieve, pressing out all the liquid.

Meanwhile, reserve about a quarter of the prawns, then purée the remainder or rub them through a fine sieve. Mix the sieved prawns with the breadcrumbs from the bread roll.

Ladle about a quarter of the fish stock over the crumb mixture and set aside; pour the remaining stock into a clean saucepan. Add the strained prawn and tomato stock and bring to the boil. Reduce the heat so that the soup simmers. Gradually stir in the soaked bread mixture. Add the vermicelli and cover the pan. Simmer for 5 minutes, or until the vermicelli is tender.

Stir in the anchovy essence or mushroom ketchup. Taste the soup and add more salt and pepper if required. Stir in the reserved whole prawns and heat through before serving.

SERVES 4

Fennel and Tomato Soup

FOOD VALUES	TOTAL	PER PORTION
Protein	15g	3g
Carbohydrate	33g	6g
Fat	33g	6g
Fibre	14g	2g
kcals	480	80

30 ml / 2 tbsp oil
1 small onion, finely
 chopped
2 fennel bulbs
4 tomatoes, peeled and
 chopped
1.5 litres / 2¾ pints
 Chicken Stock (page 44)
salt and pepper

Heat the oil in a large heavy-bottomed saucepan, add the onion and fry over gentle heat for 5 minutes.

Cut off any feathery fronds from the fennel and set them aside for the garnish. Slice the fennel bulbs into quarters, cut away the core, and roughly chop the flesh. Add the chopped fennel to the pan and fry over gentle heat for 10 minutes, turning frequently, until soft.

Add the tomatoes and chicken stock, with salt and pepper to taste. Bring the stock to the boil, lower the heat and simmer for 15-20 minutes until the fennel is tender. Serve at once, garnished with the chopped fennel fronds.

SERVES 6

VARIATION

Creamed Fennel Soup Omit the tomato. When the fennel is tender, purée the soup in a blender or food processor. Return it to the clean pan and stir in 150 ml / ¼ pint single cream. Reheat without boiling.

Brilla Soup

The original recipe called for meat on the bone, the bone being subsequently used for making stock. This slightly modified version is more practical as it reduces the original cooking time by 4 hours.

FOOD VALUES	TOTAL	PER PORTION
Protein	107g	18g
Carbohydrate	74g	12g
Fat	52g	9g
Fibre	27g	5g
kcals	1168	195

450 g / 1 lb lean shin of beef, diced

3 carrots, diced

2 turnips, diced

2 large onions, chopped

1 head of celery, diced

1 large sprig of thyme

1.75 litres / 3 pints Rich Strong Stock (page 43), Vegetable Stock (page 44) or good-quality bought beef stock

salt and pepper

Place the beef, carrots, turnips, onions, celery and thyme in a large saucepan. Pour in the stock and add a little salt and pepper. Bring slowly to the boil. Use a slotted spoon to skim off any scum which rises to the surface during this initial cooking.

Reduce the heat, cover the pan and simmer the soup for 2 hours, stirring occasionally, until the meat is tender and the soup well flavoured. Taste for seasoning before serving.

SERVES 6

Prince of Wales's Soup

This soup was invented in 1859, in honour of the 18th birthday of Albert Edward, Prince of Wales. Use the smaller cup of a double-ended melon baller to shape the turnips.

FOOD VALUES	TOTAL	PER PORTION
Protein	23g	6g
Carbohydrate	104g	26g
Fat	5g	1g
Fibre	14g	4g
kcals	522	106

4 *slices of day-old white bread*
1 *litre* / 1¾ *pints Consommé* (*page* 45)
12 *young turnips, cut into balls*
salt and white pepper
1.25 *ml* / ¼ *tsp sugar*

Set the oven at 150°C / 300°F / gas 2. Cut the bread into small discs, using a small round cutter or the rounded end of a piping tube. Spread out the discs on a baking sheet; bake until golden and very crisp.

Bring the consommé to the boil in a large saucepan. Add the turnip balls, with salt, pepper and sugar to taste. Lower the heat and simmer the soup for 10-20 minutes until the turnips are tender. Serve very hot, with the rounds of baked bread.

SERVES 4

Soup Maigre

Originally, the soup was not sieved or puréed but enriched by adding an egg yolk with the vinegar. The puréed soup is refreshing and pleasing on the palate.

FOOD VALUES	TOTAL	PER PORTION
Protein	13g	3g
Carbohydrate	37g	9g
Fat	19g	5g
Fibre	11g	3g
kcals	358	90

15 ml / 1 tbsp oil
2 onions, thinly sliced
4 celery sticks, sliced
1 lettuce, shredded
3-4 tender spinach leaves, shredded
30 ml / 2 tbsp chopped parsley
1 litre / 1¾ pints Vegetable Stock or Chicken Stock (page 44)
1 blade of mace
salt and pepper
5 ml / 1 tsp cider vinegar

Heat the oil in a large saucepan, add the onions and fry over moderate heat for 5 minutes until slightly softened. Stir in the celery, lettuce and spinach. Cook for 10 minutes over gentle heat, stirring frequently to coat the vegetables in butter and prevent them from sticking to the base of the pan.

Stir in the parsley, stock and mace, with salt and pepper to taste. Simmer for 30 minutes.

Remove the blade of mace, then purée the soup in a blender or food processor. Reheat and sharpen with the vinegar. Taste for seasoning before serving.

SERVES 4

FREEZER TIP

The puréed soup freezes very well and the recipe provides an excellent way of using a glut of home-grown lettuce. Add the vinegar after thawing and reheating. The frozen soup will keep for up to 6 months.

Mixed Vegetable Soup

Hearty vegetable soups make nutritious main meals. For extra food value and a meaty flavour, add a small piece of beef shin, smoked ham or chicken to the soup. Increase the cooking time if necessary so that the meat or poultry is very tender.

FOOD VALUES	TOTAL	PER PORTION
Protein	34g	6g
Carbohydrate	200g	34g
Fat	39g	7g
Fibre	46g	8g
kcals	1236	206

30 ml / 2 tbsp oil
1 onion, chopped
2 leeks, trimmed, sliced and washed
3 celery sticks, sliced
2 potatoes, diced
2 carrots, diced
1 swede, diced
1 parsnip, diced
1.75 litres / 3 pints Chicken Stock or Vegetable Stock (page 44)
salt and pepper

Heat the oil in a large, heavy-bottomed saucepan. Add the onion and leeks. Cook gently for 10 minutes, stirring occasionally. Add the remaining vegetables, pour in the stock and add salt and pepper to taste. Bring to the boil, lower the heat and cover the pan. Simmer for about 1 hour or until all the vegetables are tender and the soup is well flavoured.

If a clear soup with identifiable vegetables is preferred, serve at once. To thicken the soup, purée it in a blender or food processor, return to the pan and reheat.

SERVES 6

PRESSURE COOKER TIP

Put the vegetables in the cooker with only 1 litre / 1¾ pints of stock; the cooker should not be more than half full. Put the lid on the cooker and bring to 15 lb pressure. Cook for 5 minutes. Reduce pressure quickly. Add more stock if liked.

Green Pea Soup

FOOD VALUES	TOTAL	PER PORTION
Protein	61g	15g
Carbohydrate	98g	25g
Fat	24g	6g
Fibre	35g	9g
kcals	826	207

675 g / 1½ lb peas in the pod
15 ml / 1 tbsp butter or oil
1 onion, chopped
1 litre / 1¾ pints Chicken Stock or Vegetable Stock (page 44)
salt and pepper
3-4 fresh young spinach leaves, roughly chopped
1 mint sprig
2-3 parsley sprigs
pinch of sugar (optional)
60 ml / 4 tbsp plain yogurt

GARNISH
60 ml / 4 tbsp young fresh or frozen peas
4 small mint sprigs

Shell the peas, reserving about half the pods (the youngest and most tender). Melt the butter or heat the oil in a large saucepan. Add the onion and cook over gentle heat for 3-4 minutes. Add the pea pods, turning them over until coated in the butter, and cook gently for 10 minutes.

Stir in the stock, with salt and pepper to taste. Bring to the boil, then lower the heat and add the peas, spinach leaves, mint and parsley. Simmer for 10-20 minutes or until the peas are just tender.

Purée the soup in a blender or food processor, or rub through a sieve into a clean pan. Check the seasoning and add more salt and pepper if required. A pinch of sugar may also be added to bring out the flavour of the peas.

Reheat the soup to just below boiling point. In a separate pan, cook the peas for the garnish in salted boiling water until tender. Remove the soup from the heat, swirl in the yogurt and serve in individual bowls. Using a slotted spoon, ladle 15 ml / 1 tbsp freshly cooked peas into each bowl. Complete the garnish by adding the mint.

SERVES 4

Parsnip Soup

FOOD VALUES	TOTAL	PER PORTION
Protein	33g	8g
Carbohydrate	84g	21g
Fat	38g	10g
Fibre	24g	6g
kcals	791	198

15 ml / 1 tbsp oil
1 onion, chopped
450 g / 1 lb parsnips, sliced
1 litre / 1¾ pints Chicken
   Stock or Vegetable Stock
   (page 44)
salt and cayenne pepper
150 ml / ¼ pint fromage
   frais
30 ml / 2 tbsp pine nuts
   (optional)

Heat the oil in a large saucepan, add the onion and parsnips, and cook over gentle heat for 10 minutes, turning frequently to coat them in the oil.

Add the stock, with salt and cayenne to taste. Bring to the boil, lower the heat and simmer for 20 minutes until the parsnips are very soft.

Purée the soup in a blender or food processor, or rub through a sieve into a clean pan. Reheat it to just below boiling point, then stir in most of the fromage frais, reserving about 30 ml / 2 tbsp for the garnish.

Meanwhile spread out the pine nuts (if used) in a grill pan and toast them under a hot grill until golden. Ladle the soup into individual bowls and top each portion with a swirl of fromage frais and a sprinkling of toasted pine nuts.

SERVES 4

VARIATION

Spiced Parsnip Soup Add 5 ml / 1 tsp good-quality curry powder to the onion and parsnips when cooking in the oil. Substitute plain yogurt for the fromage frais and use roughly chopped cashew nuts instead of the pine nuts. Sprinkle with a little chopped fresh coriander leaves, if liked.

Leek and Oat Broth

FOOD VALUES	TOTAL	PER PORTION
Protein	29g	7g
Carbohydrate	42g	11g
Fat	6g	2g
Fibre	12g	3g
kcals	326	81

1 litre / 1¾ pints Chicken
   Stock or Vegetable Stock
   (page 44)
3 leeks, trimmed, sliced and
   washed
1 bay leaf
salt and pepper
60 ml / 4 tbsp fine or
   medium oatmeal
150 ml / ¼ pint fromage
   frais

Bring the stock and leeks to the boil in a large
saucepan. Add the bay leaf and salt and pepper to
taste. Lower the heat and simmer for 20 minutes.

Sprinkle the oatmeal into the simmering soup,
whisking all the time and simmer for 5 minutes
more. Then cover and simmer gently for a further
15-20 minutes, until thickened. Stir in the fromage
frais and serve at once.

SERVES 4

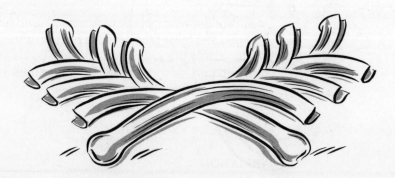

MRS BEETON'S TIP

Quick-cook porridge oats may be substituted for oatmeal and the soup
simmered for just 5 minutes before adding the fromage frais.

CANAPES AND FIRST COURSES

Garlanded Asparagus

FOOD VALUES	TOTAL	PER PORTION
Protein	43g	11g
Carbohydrate	7g	2g
Fat	64g	16g
Fibre	7g	2g
kcals	773	193

30 *asparagus spears*
salt and pepper
50 *g / 2 oz Parmesan cheese,*
 grated
25 *g / 1 oz butter*
4 *egg yolks, unbroken*

Set the oven at 200°C / 400°F / gas 6. Prepare and cook the asparagus (see page 21). Drain thoroughly and place in an ovenproof dish. Sprinkle with salt and pepper to taste. Top with the Parmesan. Bake for 15 minutes or until the cheese is golden brown.

Meanwhile, melt the butter in a frying pan over gentle heat. Add the egg yolks, and cook gently until just set outside, basting often. Using an egg slice, arrange them around the asparagus.

SERVES 4

Asparagus Rolls

FOOD VALUES	TOTAL	PER PORTION
Protein	40g	10g
Carbohydrate	130g	33g
Fat	51g	13g
Fibre	22g	6g
kcals	1105	276

12 *thin slices of wholemeal*
 bread, crusts removed
50 *g / 2 oz butter, softened*
12 *cold cooked asparagus*
 spears
salt and pepper

Flatten the bread slices lightly with a rolling pin. Spread them with butter. Lay an asparagus spear diagonally across each slice of bread. Season to taste, then roll up. Arrange the rolls in a shallow dish, seams underneath. Cover with cling film until required.

SERVES 4

Creamy Mushrooms

FOOD VALUES	TOTAL	PER PORTION (6)
Protein	19g	3g
Carbohydrate	21g	4g
Fat	24g	4g
Fibre	6g	1g
kcals	365	61

25 g / 1 oz butter
450 g / 1 lb small button
   mushrooms
10 ml / 2 tsp arrowroot
125 ml / 4 fl oz Chicken
   Stock or Vegetable Stock
   (page 44)
15 ml / 1 tbsp lemon juice
30 ml / 2 tbsp fromage frais
salt and pepper
30 ml / 2 tbsp chopped
   parsley

Melt the butter in large frying pan, add the mushrooms and fry over gentle heat without browning for 10 minutes.

Put the arrowroot in a small bowl. Stir in 30 ml / 2 tbsp of the stock until smooth. Add the remaining stock to the mushrooms and bring to the boil. Lower the heat and simmer gently for 15 minutes, stirring occasionally. Stir in the arrowroot mixture, bring to the boil, stirring, then remove the pan from the heat.

Stir in the lemon juice and fromage frais, with salt and pepper to taste. Serve sprinkled with parsley.

SERVES 4 TO 6

NUTRITION NOTE

Low-fat soft cheese may be substituted for the butter when making the asparagus rolls (left) – the result is deliciously creamy. Finely snipped fresh chives may be sprinkled sparingly over the cheese for a hint of extra flavour.

Aubergine Dip

Aubergine shells are used as containers for this richly-flavoured dip.

FOOD VALUES	TOTAL	PER PORTION
Protein	14g	2g
Carbohydrate	52g	7g
Fat	78g	10g
Fibre	17g	2g
kcals	947	106

2 small aubergines
75 ml / 3 fl oz olive oil
1 large onion, finely chopped
2 garlic cloves, crushed
100 g / 4 oz mushrooms,
  chopped
1 small green pepper, seeded
  and chopped
1 (397 g / 14 oz) can
  chopped tomatoes with
  herbs, sieved or puréed
250 ml / 8 fl oz tomato juice
15 ml / 1 tbsp red wine
  vinegar
5 ml / 1 tsp caster sugar
salt and pepper

Cut the aubergines in half lengthways. Scoop out the flesh, leaving the shells intact. Pack the shells on top of each other. Wrap closely in cling film. Refrigerate until required.

Make the dip. Cube the aubergine flesh. Heat the oil in a large frying pan. Add the onion and aubergines and fry for 5 minutes over moderate heat. Stir in the garlic, mushrooms and green pepper. Stir fry for 5 minutes.

Purée the chopped tomatoes, with their juices, in a blender or food processor. Alternatively, press them through a sieve into a bowl. Add the tomato purée to the pan with the tomato juice, vinegar and sugar. Bring to the boil, lower the heat and simmer, uncovered, for 20-30 minutes, stirring occasionally. Add salt and pepper to taste. When the mixture is very thick, remove it from the heat. Cool, then chill until required.

To serve, unwrap the aubergine shells and arrange them on a serving platter. Fill each shell with the aubergine mixture, piling it up in the centre. Serve with Melba toast, crackers or chunks of French bread.

SERVES 8

Ratatouille

Traditionally, the vegetable mixture is cooked gently for about 45-60 minutes and it is richer, and more intensely flavoured if prepared ahead, cooled and thoroughly reheated. This recipe suggests cooking for slightly less time, so that the courgettes and aubergines still retain a bit of bite; the final simmering time may be shortened, if liked, to give a mixture in which the courgettes contribute a slightly crunchy texture.

FOOD VALUES	TOTAL	PER PORTION
Protein	26g	4g
Carbohydrate	82g	12g
Fat	158g	26g
Fibre	34g	6g
kcals	1825	304

2 aubergines
salt and pepper
125-150 ml / 4-5 fl oz
  olive oil
2 large onions, finely
  chopped
2 garlic cloves, crushed
2 peppers, seeded and cut
  into thin strips
30 ml / 2 tbsp chopped fresh
  marjoram or 10 ml / 2 tsp
  dried marjoram
450 g / 1 lb tomatoes, peeled
  and chopped
4 courgettes, thinly sliced
30 ml / 2 tbsp finely chopped
  parsley or mint

Trim the aubergines and cut them into cubes. Place in a colander and sprinkle generously with salt. Set aside for 30 minutes, then rinse thoroughly, drain and pat dry on absorbent kitchen paper.

Heat some of the oil in a large saucepan or flameproof casserole, add some of the aubergine cubes and cook over moderate heat, stirring frequently, for 10 minutes. Using a slotted spoon, transfer the aubergine to a bowl; repeat until all the cubes are cooked, adding more oil as necessary. Add the onions to the oil remaining in the pan and fry for 5 minutes, until slightly softened. Stir in the garlic, peppers and marjoram, with salt and pepper to taste. Cook, stirring occasionally for 15-20 minutes, or until the onions are softened.

Stir the tomatoes and courgettes into the vegetable mixture. Replace the aubergines, heat until bubbling, then cover and simmer for a further 15-20 minutes, stirring occasionally. Serve hot, sprinkled with parsley, or cold, sprinkled with mint.

SERVES 4 TO 6

SIMPLE VEGETABLE STARTERS

Vegetables are ideal ingredients for making quick, light and healthy first courses. Select produce in peak condition, preferably purchased or picked on the day you intend serving it, then prepare and cook it simply for serving hot or cold. A simple dressing, such as a vinaigrette, complements cold vegetables. Instead of coating hot vegetables with melted butter, try serving soft cheese or fromage frais with chives. The following are a few suggestions, many of which may be adapted to suit other vegetables in season.

Dressed Artichokes Prepare and cook globe artichokes, allowing one per person (see page 20) and cover until cold. Spoon a little diced peeled and seeded tomato into each vegetable. Sprinkle with snipped chives and a little chopped mint, then dress with a little vinaigrette. Serve extra vinaigrette into which the leaf bases may be dipped before they are eaten.

Asparagus with Lemon Dressing Mix 5 ml / 1 tsp finely grated lemon rind with 300 ml / ½ pint fromage frais. Add a little finely chopped parsley and salt and pepper to taste. Serve with hot or cold asparagus, offering thinly sliced light rye bread as an accompaniment.

Beetroot with Egg Garnish Serve diced cooked beetroot, tossed in a little olive oil and a squeeze of lemon juice, topped with chopped hard-boiled egg and sprinkled with chopped fresh dill.

Beetroot with Horseradish As a dip or spread to serve with crackers or savoury biscuits, mix grated cooked beetroot with a little low-fat soft cheese and sufficient plain yogurt to just bind the mixture to a soft spreading consistency. Stir in horseradish sauce, salt and pepper to taste. Serve in a bowl, surrounded by warmed water biscuits, or spoon in neat piles on bases of shredded lettuce on individual plates.

Broccoli with Walnuts Freshly picked purple sprouting broccoli makes a splendid starter. Steam or boil the tender spears (see page 23). Heat a small knob of butter with a little olive oil, add some chopped walnuts – make sure they are good quality and fresh – and heat for a few minutes. Spoon the nuts over the broccoli and serve with wholemeal bread and butter.

Carrot Starter Coarsely grate fresh young carrots, toss them with a trickle of light salad oil, a little lemon or orange juice and seasoning to taste. Add some snipped chives if you like or serve plain – excellent with home-baked bread rolls.

Celeriac Starter Coarsely grated or finely shredded celeriac makes a light first-course salad as for carrots (left). Toss the celeriac in lemon juice as soon as it is prepared to prevent it from discolouring. Dress with a little fromage frais and toss in some chopped dill. Season to taste, pile on individual plates and garnish with chopped hard-boiled egg and sliced cocktail gherkins. Serve with dark rye bread or pumpernickel.

Celery Canapés Flavour low-fat soft cheese with finely chopped herbs; pipe along short lengths of celery stick. Top with walnut pieces, sliced green or black olives or short strips of drained canned or bottled pimiento.

Cherry Tomatoes with a Simple Dip Mix snipped chives, a little chopped parsley and freshly grated Parmesan cheese into low-fat soft cheese. Stir in a little yogurt to soften the cheese to a dipping consistency and add salt and pepper to taste. Serve surrounded by cherry tomatoes. Leave the stalks on the tomatoes so that they are easy to pick up and dip; then the tomatoes can be eaten off the stalks.

Corn-on-the-cob Freshly cooked corn may be served with a dressing of low-fat soft cheese and snipped chives or fromage frais mixed with finely chopped walnuts and spring onion instead of butter. A satisfying first course or tempting light supper.

Mushroom Bites Heat some olive oil and a crushed clove of garlic in a large frying pan. Toss small button mushrooms in the hot oil for a few minutes over high heat, then use a slotted spoon to remove them from the pan. Sprinkle with a little grated Parmesan cheese, salt and pepper, and chopped parsley. Pierce each mushroom with a cocktail stick and serve on the canapé tray. They are good hot or cold.

Filled Tomatoes Mix finely chopped cooked ham and a little chopped spring onion with low-fat soft cheese. Add salt and pepper to taste. Soften the mixture with a little fromage frais, if necessary, then pipe it into scooped-out small tomatoes. Serve two per person as a first course, or fill cherry tomatoes to serve on a mixed canapé tray.

Vegetables Vinaigrette Hot or cold vegetables, such as globe artichokes, asparagus, broad beans, carrots, salad greens or new potatoes, taste delicious with a simple Vinaigrette Dressing (page 122). Alternatively, use Chiffonade Dressing (page 123). This is particularly good with lightly cooked French beans, asparagus or broccoli.

Potted Mushrooms

Serve full-flavoured potted mushrooms with crusty bread or thick slices of Granary bread if you plan a substantial first course, or offer thin Melba toast if a light starter is more suitable.

FOOD VALUES	TOTAL	PER PORTION
Protein	11g	3g
Carbohydrate	2g	–
Fat	45g	11g
Fibre	5g	1g
kcals	455	114

450 g / 1 lb mushrooms, finely chopped
50 g / 2 oz butter
salt and pepper
pinch of ground allspice
2 anchovy fillets, mashed finely

Place the mushrooms in a heavy-bottomed saucepan over gentle heat until the juice runs freely. Raise the heat and cook, uncovered, stirring often until all the juice evaporates and the mushrooms are dry.

Add the butter with salt and pepper to taste. Sprinkle with the allspice and continue cooking for about 5 minutes, or until all the butter is absorbed.

Stir in the anchovies and cook for 2 minutes more. Remove from the heat, turn into small pots and leave to cool. Cover and chill for at least an hour before serving.

SERVES 4

MAIN DISHES

Haddock Florentine

FOOD VALUES	TOTAL	PER PORTION
Protein	240g	60g
Carbohydrate	55g	14g
Fat	114g	29g
Fibre	23g	6g
kcals	2263	566

1 kg / 2¼ lb fresh spinach
25 g / 1 oz butter
salt and pepper
100 ml / 3½ fl oz Fish Stock
  (page 42)
100 ml / 3½ fl oz dry white
  wine
1 kg / 2¼ lb haddock fillets,
  skinned, cut in portions
pinch of grated nutmeg
50 g / 2 oz Parmesan cheese,
  grated

MORNAY SAUCE
1 small onion
1 small carrot
1 small celery stick
600 ml / 1 pint milk
1 bay leaf
few parsley stalks
1 fresh thyme sprig
1 clove
6 white peppercorns
1 blade of mace
40 g / 1½ oz butter
50 g / 2 oz plain flour
1 egg yolk
25 g / 1 oz Gruyère cheese,
  grated
25 g / 1 oz Parmesan cheese,
  grated
pinch of grated nutmeg

Start by making the sauce. Combine the onion, carrot, celery and milk in a saucepan. Add the herbs and spices, with salt to taste. Heat to simmering point, cover, turn off the heat and allow to stand for 30 minutes to infuse. Strain into a measuring jug.

Melt the butter in a saucepan. Stir in the flour and cook over low heat for 2-3 minutes, stirring occasionally, without allowing the mixture to colour. Gradually add the flavoured milk, stirring constantly.

Continue to cook over moderate heat, stirring until the mixture boils and thickens to a thick coating consistency. When the mixture boils, lower the heat and simmer gently for 1-2 minutes, stirring occasionally to prevent the formation of a skin.

Beat the egg yolk in a small bowl. Add a little of the sauce and mix well. Add the contents of the bowl to the sauce and heat gently, stirring. Do not allow the sauce to boil. Stir in the cheeses until melted. Add the nutmeg. Cover the surface of the sauce closely with damp greaseproof paper and set aside.

Tear the spinach leaves from the stalks and place in a large saucepan with the butter. Add salt and pepper to taste. Cover with a tight-fitting lid and cook gently for about 15 minutes, shaking the pan occasionally. Meanwhile, combine the stock and white wine in a large saucepan. Bring to simmering point, add the fish and poach for 7-10 minutes.

Drain the spinach thoroughly in a colander, pressing out all free liquid with the back of a wooden spoon. Put the spinach on the base of a lightly greased baking dish. Remove the fish portions with a slotted spoon and arrange them on top of the spinach. Keep hot.

Boil the fish and wine stock until reduced by half. Reheat the sauce, stirring frequently. Add the reduced stock, season with salt, pepper and nutmeg and pour the sauce over the fish. Sprinkle with the grated Parmesan and brown under a hot grill. Serve at once.

SERVES 4

Poultry with Peas

FOOD VALUES	TOTAL	PER PORTION
Protein	125g	31g
Carbohydrate	68g	17g
Fat	51g	13g
Fibre	22g	6g
kcals	1211	303

350 g / 12 oz cooked meat from chicken, turkey, duck or goose, cut in neat pieces
salt and pepper
2.5 ml / ½ tsp ground mace
30 ml / 2 tbsp plain flour
30 ml / 2 tbsp oil
300 ml / ½ pint poultry or giblet stock
450 g / 1 lb shelled peas
5 ml / 1 tsp sugar

Place the poultry in a small bowl. Add plenty of salt and pepper, the mace and flour. Toss well to coat. Heat the oil in a heavy-bottomed saucepan. Add the poultry, reserving any flour in the bowl, and brown the pieces lightly.

Stir in any remaining flour, then gradually pour in the stock and bring to the boil, stirring. Add the peas, reduce the heat so that the sauce simmers and cover the pan. Cook for 20 minutes, until the peas are tender. Stir in the sugar and check the seasoning. Serve with rice or noodles, if liked.

SERVES 4

Duck with Turnips

FOOD VALUES	TOTAL	PER PORTION (4)
Protein	161g	40g
Carbohydrate	60g	15g
Fat	248g	62g
Fibre	20g	5g
kcals	3172	793

30 ml / 2 tbsp oil
1 (2.25 kg / 5 lb) duck
salt
1 bouquet garni
6 black peppercorns
2 cloves
about 600 ml / 1 pint well-
    flavoured duck or chicken
    stock
450 g / 1 lb young turnips,
    sliced
75 ml / 5 tbsp medium-dry
    sherry (optional)

MIREPOIX
2 onions, sliced
2 carrots, sliced
1 small turnip, sliced
1 celery stick, sliced

Heat half the oil in a large saucepan. Stir in the mirepoix ingredients. Lay the duck on the vegetables, cover the pan and cook very gently for 20 minutes, shaking the pan occasionally. Add salt, the bouquet garni and spices, then pour in enough stock to cover three quarters of the mirepoix. Cover the pan with foil and a tight-fitting lid. Simmer gently for 1¼ hours, adding more stock if necessary.

Heat the remaining oil in a frying pan, add the turnips and toss over moderate heat for 4-5 minutes, then add to the duck and cook for 45 minutes, until the duck is tender. Set the oven at 220°C / 425°F / gas 7. Put a baking sheet in the oven to heat up.

Remove the duck from the pan, place it on the hot baking sheet and put it in the oven for 10 minutes to crisp the skin. Using a slotted spoon, transfer the turnips to a heated bowl. Keep hot. Remove the excess fat from the top of the stock. Strain it into a clean pan, boil it until reduced by half, and stir in the sherry, if used. Serve the duck on a hot platter, with the turnips. Offer the sauce separately.

SERVES 4 TO 5

Duck and Red Cabbage

The trimmings from two roast ducks should yield enough meat
for this flavoursome dish.

FOOD VALUES	TOTAL	PER PORTION (6)
Protein	108g	18g
Carbohydrate	38g	6g
Fat	60g	10g
Fibre	9g	2g
kcals	1121	187

25 g / 1 oz butter
450 g / 1 lb red cabbage,
   shredded
salt and pepper
well-flavoured stock (see
   method)
about 400 g / 14 oz cold
   roast duck, shredded
15 ml / 1 tbsp red wine
   vinegar
15 ml / 1 tbsp demerara
   sugar

Melt the butter in a heavy-bottomed saucepan and add the red cabbage. Stir lightly to coat the cabbage in butter, then add salt and pepper. Cover the pan tightly and simmer for 1 hour. Shake the pan from time to time to prevent the cabbage from sticking to the base, and add just enough stock to prevent it from burning.

In another pan, combine the duck with enough stock to moisten. Place over gentle heat until the duck is heated through. Add the vinegar and sugar to the cabbage, mix well, then turn on to a heated dish. Drain the duck and arrange it on the top. Serve with a mixture of brown rice and wild rice, if liked.

SERVES 4 TO 6

NUTRITION NOTE

Ducks are now bred to be leaner than their wild relations and this is particularly noticeable when roasting a whole bird or buying breast fillets complete with skin. Skinned duck portions (breast fillets or quarters) may be used in the recipe opposite instead of the whole bird to reduce the fat content to a minimum. Reduce the initial cooking time to 30 minutes instead of 1¼ hours. Since the skin has been removed, there is no need to brown the portions before serving them.

Duck with Green Peas

FOOD VALUES	TOTAL	PER PORTION (4)
Protein	258g	65g
Carbohydrate	143g	36g
Fat	335g	84g
Fibre	52g	13g
kcals	4577	1144

1 kg / 2¼ lb fresh peas
12 button onions, peeled but left whole
15 g / ½ oz butter
225 g / 8 oz rindless bacon rashers, halved
1 (2.25 kg / 5 lb) duck
450 ml / ¾ pint Chicken Stock (page 44)
1 bouquet garni
salt and pepper

Set the oven at 180°C / 350°F / gas 4. Shell the peas and set them aside. Bring a small saucepan of water to the boil, add the onions and cook for 2-3 minutes. Drain thoroughly.

Melt the butter in a large flameproof casserole, add the onions and bacon and stir fry until the onions are pale brown and the bacon is beginning to crisp. Using a slotted spoon, set the onions and bacon aside. Add the duck to the fat remaining in the casserole. Brown it quickly on all sides over moderate heat, then carefully lift it out of the pan. Put on a plate and reserve. Pour away the fat from the casserole, add a third of the stock and boil down to half its quantity, then add the rest of the stock.

Return the duck to the casserole and stir in the reserved onions and bacon. Add the bouquet garni and season lightly with salt and pepper. Bring to the boil, then cover the casserole and transfer it to the oven. Bake for 1¼ hours. Stir in the peas. Replace the cover, return the casserole to the oven and bake for about 45 minutes more or until the duck is cooked through and the peas are tender, basting occasionally.

Using a slotted spoon, transfer the duck, peas, onions and bacon to a serving dish; keep hot. Skim off any fat from the surface of the liquid, then boil until reduced to a coating sauce. Pour over the duck and serve.

SERVES 4 TO 5

Stuffed Cabbage Leaves

FOOD VALUES	TOTAL	PER PORTION
Protein	86g	22g
Carbohydrate	54g	14g
Fat	82g	21g
Fibre	11g	3g
kcals	1282	321

fat for greasing
8 large cabbage leaves

STUFFING AND SAUCE
15 ml / 1 tbsp oil
1 onion, finely chopped
400 g / 14 oz lean minced beef
1 (397 g / 14 oz) can tomatoes
30 ml / 2 tbsp cornflour
15 ml / 1 tbsp Worcestershire sauce
2.5 ml / ½ tsp dried mixed herbs
15 ml / 1 tbsp chopped parsley
salt and pepper
15 ml / 1 tbsp tomato purée

Remove the thick central stems from the cabbage leaves, then blanch them in boiling water for 2 minutes. Drain well. To make the stuffing, heat the oil in a saucepan and gently fry the onion for 5 minutes. Add the beef and cook, stirring, until the meat has browned. Drain the tomatoes and reserve the juice. Roughly chop the tomatoes and add them to the meat mixture. Mix 10 ml (2 tsp) of the cornflour with the Worcestershire sauce in a cup; stir into the meat mixture with the herbs and salt and pepper. Cover and cook for 20 minutes, stirring occasionally.

Grease a shallow ovenproof dish. Set the oven at 190°C / 375°F / gas 5. Divide the stuffing between the cabbage leaves and roll up, folding over the edges of the leaves to enclose the meat completely. Place in the prepared dish and cover with foil. Bake for 20 minutes.

Meanwhile make the sauce. Mix the reserved juice from the tomatoes with the tomato purée in a measuring jug; make up to 250 ml / 8 fl oz with water. In a cup, blend the remaining cornflour with 15 ml / 1 tbsp of the sauce. Pour the rest of the sauce into a saucepan and bring to the boil. Stir in the blended cornflour. Boil, stirring all the time, until the sauce has thickened. Add salt and pepper to taste. Pour the sauce over the stuffed cabbage leaves just before serving.

SERVES 4

Boiled Beef and Dumplings

Old-fashioned dishes, such as this one, often highlight the traditional role of vegetables in the British diet. A modest joint of meat would be surrounded by generous quantities of seasonal vegetables and hearty dumplings to satisfy hungry appetites. The joint itself would probably provide for two – or more – family meals, with the emphasis on eating plenty of satisfying vegetables.

FOOD VALUES	TOTAL	PER PORTION (10)
Protein	519g	52g
Carbohydrate	550g	55g
Fat	167g	17g
Fibre	68g	7g
kcals	5632	563

1-1.25 kg / 2½-2¾ lb beef brisket or silverside, trimmed of fat
5 ml / 1 tsp salt
3 cloves
10 peppercorns
1 bouquet garni
3 onions, quartered
4 potatoes, halved or quartered
4 large carrots, cut lengthways in quarters, then in thick slices
4 small turnips, halved
1 small swede, cut in chunks

DUMPLINGS
225 g / 8 oz self-raising flour
2.5 ml / ½ tsp salt
100 g / 4 oz shredded beef suet

Weigh the meat and calculate the cooking time, allowing 25 minutes per 450 g / 1 lb plus 20 minutes over. Tie the meat to a neat shape with string, if necessary. Put it into a large heavy-bottomed saucepan, cover with boiling water and add the salt. Bring to the boil again and boil for 5 minutes to seal the surface of the meat.

Lower the heat to simmering point, skim, then add the cloves, peppercorns and bouquet garni. Cover the pan and simmer for the rest of the calculated cooking time.

About 45 minutes before the end of the cooking time, add the onions; 15 minutes later add the potatoes and carrots. Make the dumplings by sifting the flour and salt into a mixing bowl. Stir in the suet and add enough cold water to make a firm elastic dough. Divide the dough into walnut-sized pieces, shaping each into a neat ball.

Twenty minutes before the end of the cooking time, add the turnips and swede, and bring the stock around the beef to boiling point. Drop in the dumplings. Lower the heat, half cover the pan and

70

simmer until the dumplings are cooked, turning them over once with a slotted spoon.

To serve, remove the dumplings from the pan and arrange them as a border on a large heated serving dish. Remove and discard the bouquet garni, then lift out the vegetables with a slotted spoon and arrange them with the dumplings, placing excess vegetables in a separate dish. Remove any strings from the meat, skewer it if necessary to retain the shape, and set it in the centre of the dish. Serve some of the cooking liquid separately in a sauceboat.

SERVES 8 TO 10

NUTRITION NOTE

Although it is not a good idea to stoke up on suet dumplings too frequently, eating larger proportions of vegetables than meat makes sound nutrition sense. Cabbage, Brussels sprouts or broccoli may also be added to the pot of boiled beef – adopt a contemporary approach and cook these vegetables until they are only just tender to retain their full food value. Their crunchy texture contrasts well with the boiled root vegetables.

Bigos

There are many ways of preparing what is in effect Poland's national dish. The essence of them all is that they should consist of a mixture of sauerkraut and smoked sausage and the game secured by the hunter. Duck or any type of game can be used instead of venison.

FOOD VALUES	TOTAL	PER PORTION
Protein	207g	52g
Carbohydrate	99g	25g
Fat	137g	34g
Fibre	18g	5g
kcals	2520	630

1 kg / 2¼ lb sauerkraut
450 g / 1 lb boneless
   shoulder of venison
175-225 g / 6-8 oz smoked
   pork sausage
40 g / 1½ oz lard or 30 ml /
   2 tbsp oil
1 large onion, sliced
30 ml / 2 tbsp tomato purée
125 ml / 4 fl oz red wine
salt and pepper
1 large green apple
2 bay leaves
250 ml / 8 fl oz Game or
   Chicken Stock (page 44)
25 g / 1 oz butter
15 ml / 1 tbsp plain flour

Thoroughly squeeze the sauerkraut, then shred it. Wipe the venison, trim off all the fat and cut into 2.5 cm / 1 inch cubes. Slice the sausage into pieces 1 cm / ½ inch thick. Melt half the lard or heat half the oil in a large frying pan and brown the onion until golden. Add the venison and cook, stirring for 5 minutes. Stir in the tomato purée and the wine. Season to taste and mix in the sausage.

Set the oven at 180°C / 350°F / gas 4. Place half the sauerkraut in a large casserole, then top with the meat mixture. Peel, core and dice the apple. Add it to the casserole with the bay leaves and place the remaining sauerkraut on top. Pour half the stock over the bigos. Dot with flakes of butter, cover and cook for 2½-3 hours. Stir occasionally.

About 10 minutes before the end of cooking time, heat the remaining lard or oil in a frying pan, add the flour and stir over low heat for 2-3 minutes, without allowing the mixture to colour. Gradually add the remaining stock, stirring all the time, until the sauce boils and thickens. Simmer for 2 minutes, stirring, then season to taste. Mix the sauce into the bigos, which should be moist. Serve piping hot.

SERVES 4

Baked Stuffed Peppers

FOOD VALUES	TOTAL	PER PORTION
Protein	87g	21g
Carbohydrate	66g	17g
Fat	68g	17g
Fibre	15g	4g
kcals	1201	300

fat for greasing
4 green peppers
1 small onion, finely
  chopped
400 g / 14 oz lean minced
  beef
100 g / 4 oz cooked rice
salt and pepper
good pinch of dried
  marjoram
250 ml / 8 fl oz tomato juice
strips of green pepper to
  garnish

Grease an ovenproof dish large enough to hold all the peppers snugly in an upright position. Set the oven at 180°C / 350°F / gas 4. Cut a slice off the top of each pepper, then remove the membranes and seeds. Blanch in a saucepan of boiling water for 2 minutes.

Mix the onion, beef, rice, salt, pepper and marjoram together in a bowl. Stand the peppers upright in the prepared dish; if they do not stand straight, cut a thin slice off the base. Divide the stuffing mixture between the peppers. Pour the tomato juice around the base of the peppers. Cover and bake for 1 hour. Garnish with strips of pepper and serve.

SERVES 4

MRS BEETON'S TIP

Use a large Polish boiling sausage for Bigos (left), for example *wiejska*, available from larger supermarkets and delicatessens. The sauerkraut is usually squeezed and shredded before being added to the stew; however, if preferred it may be rinsed and squeezed first. Another traditional ingredient is dried mushrooms: soak 2-4 in boiling water to cover for 15 minutes, then drain and chop them before adding to the bigos at the beginning of cooking. Strain the soaking water through muslin and add that too.

Couscous

FOOD VALUES	TOTAL	PER PORTION
Protein	147g	18g
Carbohydrate	406g	51g
Fat	170g	21g
Fibre	34g	4g
kcals	3643	455

50 g / 2 oz chick-peas
45 ml / 3 tbsp olive oil
8 chicken thighs, skinned
2 garlic cloves, crushed
1 large onion, chopped
1 green pepper, seeded and sliced
1 green chilli, seeded and chopped (optional)
15 ml / 1 tbsp ground coriander
5 ml / 1 tsp ground cumin
100 g / 4 oz carrots, sliced
100 g / 4 oz turnips, cut into chunks
450 g / 1 lb pumpkin, peeled, seeds removed and cut into chunks
450 g / 1 lb potatoes, cubed
1 bay leaf
2 (397 g / 14 oz) cans chopped tomatoes
50 g / 2 oz raisins
150 ml / ¼ pint Chicken Stock (page 44) or water
salt and pepper
225 g / 8 oz courgettes, sliced
45 ml / 3 tbsp chopped parsley
350 g / 12 oz couscous
50 g / 2 oz butter, melted

Soak the chick peas overnight in plenty of cold water. Drain the chick-peas, then cook them in plenty of fresh boiling water for 10 minutes. Lower the heat, cover the pan and simmer for 1½ hours, or until the chick-peas are just tender. Drain.

Heat the oil in a very large flameproof casserole or saucepan. Add the chicken pieces and brown them all over, then use a slotted spoon to remove them from the pan and set aside. Add the garlic, onion, pepper and chilli, if used, to the oil remaining in the pan and cook for 5 minutes, stirring.

Stir in the coriander and cumin, then add the carrots, turnips, pumpkin, potatoes, bay leaf, tomatoes, raisins and stock or water with salt and pepper to taste. Stir in the drained chick-peas. Bring to the boil, then lower the heat and replace the chicken thighs, tucking them in among the vegetables. Cover and simmer gently for 1 hour. Stir in the courgettes and parsley, cover the pan and continue to cook gently for a further 30 minutes.

There are two options for preparing the couscous The first is to line a steamer with scalded muslin, then sprinkle the couscous into it. Place the steamer over the simmering stew for the final 30 minutes' cooking, covering it tightly to keep all the steam in. Alternatively – and this is the easier method – place the couscous in a deep casserole or bowl and pour in fresh boiling water from the kettle to cover the grains by 2.5 cm / 1 inch. Cover and set aside for 15 minutes. The grains will absorb the boiling water and swell. If the couscous cools on standing, it may be reheated over a pan of boiling water or in a microwave for about 2 minutes on High.

To serve, transfer the couscous to a very large serving dish and pour the hot melted butter over it. Fork up the grains and make a well in the middle. Ladle the chicken and vegetable stew into the well, spooning cooking juices over the couscous.

SERVES 8

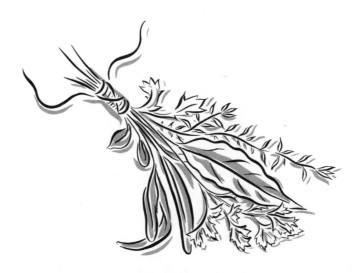

MRS BEETON'S TIP

Cubes of boneless lamb may be used instead of the chicken. The vegetables may be varied according to what is freshly available – marrow or green beans may be added or substituted for other ingredients.

Couscous is usually accompanied by a hot, spicy condiment known as *harissa*. This paste, made from chillies, cumin, coriander, garlic, mint and oil, is deep red in colour and fiery of flavour. It is added to individual portions to taste but should be treated with respect.

Spiced Lentils

Serve these spiced lentils with brown basmati rice and a mixed vegetable curry or side dish or spicy spinach to make a tempting vegetarian meal. Along with other beans and pulses, vegetables and grains, lentils are a valuable source of protein in a vegetarian diet.

FOOD VALUES	TOTAL	PER PORTION (6)
Protein	111g	19g
Carbohydrate	288g	48g
Fat	52g	9g
Fibre	29g	5g
kcals	1990	332

450 g / 1 lb red lentils
2.5 ml / ½ tsp sea salt
45 ml / 3 tbsp oil
1 onion, chopped
1 small cooking apple, chopped
1.25 ml / ¼ tsp turmeric
1.25 ml / ¼ tsp ground ginger
5 ml / 1 tsp garam masala
5 ml / 1 tsp ground cumin
3 tomatoes, peeled and chopped

GARNISH
chopped fresh coriander leaves
chopped onion or fried onion rings

Put the lentils in a large saucepan with 900 ml / 1½ pints water. Bring to the boil, lower the heat and cover the pan. Simmer gently for 20 minutes. Add the sea salt and simmer for 5 minutes more or until the lentils are soft and all the water has been absorbed.

Meanwhile, heat the oil in a large deep frying pan and add the onion, apple and spices. Fry gently for about 10 minutes until the onion and apple are soft and lightly browned. Stir the tomatoes into the pan and cook for 5 minutes, then pour in the lentils.

Stir thoroughly, then serve very hot, sprinkled with the coriander leaves and onion.

SERVES 4 TO 6

MRS BEETON'S TIP

To peel tomatoes, cut a small cross in the top of each fruit and place them in a bowl. Pour on freshly boiling water. Leave for about 45 seconds, depending on ripeness, then drain. Peel back and remove the skins.

Lentil Pasties

Serve a crisp salad and new potatoes with these pasties to make a satisfying summer meal or offer baked potatoes and Ratatouille (page 59) for a warming winter menu.

FOOD VALUES	TOTAL	PER PASTY
Protein	55g	7g
Carbohydrate	236g	29g
Fat	123g	15g
Fibre	13g	2g
kcals	2212	277

100 g / 4 oz red lentils
300 ml / ½ pint Vegetable
   Stock (page 44)
25 g / 1 oz butter
salt and pepper
pinch of grated nutmeg
4 button mushrooms, sliced
15 ml / 1 tbsp double cream
beaten egg or milk for
   glazing

SHORT CRUST PASTRY
225 g / 8 oz plain flour
2.5 ml / ½ tsp salt
100 g / 4 oz margarine
flour for rolling out

Make the pastry. Sift the flour and salt into a bowl, then rub in the margarine until the mixture resembles fine breadcrumbs. Add enough cold water to make a stiff dough. Press the dough together with your fingertips. Wrap in greaseproof paper and chill until required.

Put the lentils in a saucepan with the vegetable stock. Bring to the boil, lower the heat and cover the pan. Simmer for 20 minutes or until the lentils are soft and all the liquid is absorbed. Beat in the butter and season with salt, pepper and nutmeg. Stir in the mushrooms and cream. Set aside. Set the oven at 200°C / 400°F / gas 6.

Roll out the pastry very thinly on a floured surface, and cut into eight 13 cm / 5 inch rounds. Divide the lentil filling between the rounds, dampen the edges and fold over to form half circles. Press the edges together and seal firmly, then brush with a little beaten egg or milk. Place on baking sheets and bake for about 15 minutes, or until the pastry is cooked and browned.

MAKES 8

Haricot Beans with Parsley Sauce

FOOD VALUES	TOTAL	PER PORTION
Protein	60g	10g
Carbohydrate	141g	22g
Fat	50g	8g
Fibre	5g	1g
kcals	1222	204

200 g / 7 oz haricot beans, soaked overnight in cold water to cover
30 ml / 2 tbsp butter
1 onion, finely chopped
100 g / 4 oz mushrooms, thinly sliced
15 ml / 1 tbsp lemon juice
Pesto Genovese (right), to serve

PARSLEY SAUCE
25 g / 1 oz butter
25 g / 1 oz plain flour
300 ml / ½ pint milk
salt and pepper
60 ml / 4 tbsp chopped parsley

Drain the beans. Put them in a saucepan with fresh water to cover. Bring to the boil, boil vigorously for 10 minutes, then lower the heat, cover the pan and simmer for about 40 minutes or until the beans are tender.

When the beans are almost cooked, melt the butter in a small frying pan, add the onion and fry over gentle heat for 10 minutes until soft and transparent. Add the mushrooms and cook for a further 5 minutes. Set the pan aside.

Make the parsley sauce. Melt the butter in a saucepan, stir in the flour and cook for 1 minute. Gradually add the milk, stirring constantly, and cook until the mixture boils and thickens. Add salt and pepper to taste, then stir in the parsley.

Drain the haricot beans. Add them to the parsley sauce with the lemon juice. Toss together lightly. Stir in the reserved mushroom mixture, with salt and pepper to taste. Heat through gently. Serve in individual bowls, topped with pesto.

SERVES 6

Pesto Genovese

A little pesto goes a long way to flavour pasta. Put the pasta in a heated serving bowl or individual dishes, add the pesto and toss lightly. Serve at once.

FOOD VALUES	TOTAL	PER PORTION
Protein	21g	5g
Carbohydrate	3g	1g
Fat	131g	33g
Fibre	2g	1g
kcals	1273	318

2 *garlic cloves, roughly chopped*
25-40 *g / 1-1½ oz fresh basil leaves, roughly chopped*
25 *g / 1 oz pine nuts, chopped*
40 *g / 1 oz Parmesan cheese, grated*
juice of 1 lemon
salt and pepper
75-100 *ml / 3-3½ fl oz olive oil*

Combine the garlic, basil leaves, nuts, Parmesan, lemon juice, salt and pepper in a mortar. Pound with a pestle until smooth. Alternatively, process in a blender or food processor. While blending, trickle in the oil as when making mayonnaise, until the sauce forms a very thick paste.

SERVES 4

79

NUTRITIOUS VEGETABLE CASSEROLES

Vegetables are essential ingredients for making successful casseroles, from the simple combination of onion and carrot to create a distinctive flavour base to rich ragouts of vegetables alone, such as ratatouille.

In the context of healthy eating, vegetables contribute far more than a flavour base for protein foods: by using them in significant quantities to extend small or modest portions of poultry and meat, the content of the meal complies with suggested guidelines for a balanced diet. Ironically, the dish of old-fashioned boiled beef and vegetables is a good example, especially if the meat is sparingly shared and made to furnish more than one meal – as it undoubtedly would have done when the recipe was an everyday favourite. Couscous is another good example of a dish which includes more vegetables and carbohydrate foods than meat.

A variety of vegetables can be added to basic casseroles which are to be served with baked potatoes, rice or pasta.

- Celery, green or red pepper, French beans and new potatoes combine well with fish and seafood casseroles.
- Jerusalem artichokes and mushrooms may be braised with chicken or turkey.
- Aubergines, peppers and onions are excellent with duck, beef, lamb or pork.
- Beetroot and chick-peas complement pork casseroles.
- Brussels sprouts and cabbage are good with bacon, pork or beef.
- Celeriac combines well with other root vegetables in all types of hot pot and when boiling bacon.
- The distinctive aniseed flavour of fennel is delicious with lamb or pork, especially when new potatoes or pasta are added to the hot pot.
- Peas, sweetcorn and courgettes are ideal for bulking out poultry casseroles and pork stews.

THE MAIN DISH VEGETABLE CASSEROLE

Many mixed vegetable casseroles are sufficiently flavoursome and substantial to stand alone as a main dish and will satisfy the meat-stew palate as well as appealing to those who already appreciate vegetarian meals. For best results, combine well-flavoured ingredients with hearty vegetables and ensure that the sauce is of exactly the right consistency. Beans and pulses add food value as well as bulk. A gratin-style topping or scone-based cobbler crust can often be used with the braised vegetables to create a substantial dish. Try the

combinations suggested below (onions, a bouquet garni and a carrot should be regarded as essential flavouring ingredients).

- Celery, carrots, parsnips, peppers and potatoes make an excellent base for a lightly curried casserole.
- Marrow, potatoes and broad beans are delicious braised with cider and tomatoes.
- Sweet potatoes, corn and courgettes make a colourful casserole; add chick-peas for their food value and nutty flavour and sharpen the sauce with a little plain yogurt.
- Braise Brussels sprouts with carrots and haricot beans, then add a topping of wholemeal breadcrumbs and grated cheese.
- Stew red kidney beans with aubergines and pumpkin, flavouring the casserole with garlic, cumin seeds and cardamoms. Serve swirled with plain yogurt and accompanied by aromatic Basmati rice.
- Make a light summer dish by braising celery, French beans and flageolet together in a little cider and stock. Add shredded Swiss chard or spinach towards the end of cooking and top with toasted pine nuts before serving.

Toppings for Vegetable Casseroles

- Breadcrumbs with grated cheese and chopped spring onion, seasoned with paprika and a little grated nutmeg. Brown under the grill or in the oven.
- Wholemeal breadcrumbs with chopped walnuts, grated orange rind, chopped thyme and parsley. Toss quickly in a little olive oil in a large frying pan until lightly browned and crisped.
- Cook pine nuts and raisins in a little olive oil until the pine nuts are lightly and evenly browned. Add a little orange juice and simmer until the raisins are plump and the juice has evaporated. Sprinkle over casseroles which include cabbage, spinach or other greens.
- Make a savoury crumble: rub 50 g / 2 oz margarine into 100 g / 4 oz plain flour, then stir in 25 g / 1 oz grated cheese, 5 ml / 1 tsp chopped thyme, 30 ml / 2 tbsp chopped parsley and 30 ml / 2 tbsp rolled oats. Season with salt and pepper and sprinkle over moist casseroles, then bake at 180°C / 350°F / gas 4 for about 45 minutes.
- For a cobbler topping, rub 50 g / 2 oz margarine into 225 g / 8 oz self-raising flour. Add 25 g / 1 oz grated cheese, 30 ml / 2 tbsp snipped chives and about 150 ml / ¼ pint milk. Mix in the milk slowly to just bind the dough. Roll it out thickly and stamp out about eight cobblers (scones) or divide it into eight portions and flatten them into round scones. Overlap the cobblers around the edge of a moist stew, brush with a little milk and bake at 190°C / 375°F / gas 5 for about 40 minutes, or until the cobblers are thoroughly cooked.

Spicy Spinach and Chick-peas

The use of canned chick-peas makes this delicious dish
a quick-cook option.

FOOD VALUES	TOTAL	PER PORTION (6)
Protein	81g	14g
Carbohydrate	146g	24g
Fat	49g	8g
Fibre	53g	9g
kcals	1320	220

25 g / 1 oz butter
30 ml / 2 tbsp cumin seeds
15 ml / 1 tbsp coriander
  seeds, crushed
15 ml / 1 tbsp mustard seeds
1 large onion, chopped
2 garlic cloves, crushed
2 (425 g / 15 oz) cans chick-
  peas, drained
5 ml / 1 tsp turmeric
1 kg / 2¼ lb fresh spinach,
  cooked
salt and pepper

Melt the butter in a saucepan, add the cumin,
coriander and mustard seeds and cook gently,
stirring, for about 3 minutes, or until the seeds
are aromatic. Keep the heat low to avoid burning
the butter.

Add the onion and garlic to the pan and continue to
cook for about 15 minutes, until the onion is
softened. Stir in the chick-peas and turmeric and
cook for 5 minutes, until thoroughly hot. Tip the
spinach into the pan and stir it over moderate heat
until heated through. Season and serve.

SERVES 4 TO 6

Soya Bean Bake

FOOD VALUES	TOTAL	PER PORTION
Protein	207g	35g
Carbohydrate	277g	46g
Fat	168g	28g
Fibre	98g	16g
kcals	3370	561

fat for greasing
450 g / 1 lb soya beans,
soaked for 24 hours in
cold water to cover
2 onions, finely chopped
1 green pepper, seeded and
chopped
1 carrot, coarsely grated
1 celery stick, sliced
45 ml / 3 tbsp molasses
45 ml / 3 tbsp chopped
parsley
5 ml / 1 tsp dried thyme
5 ml / 1 tsp dried savory or
marjoram
salt and pepper
2 (397 g / 14 oz) cans
chopped tomatoes
175 g / 6 oz medium
oatmeal
50 g / 2 oz Lancashire or
Caerphilly cheese, finely
crumbled or grated
45 ml / 3 tbsp snipped chives
50 ml / 2 fl oz olive oil

Grease a large ovenproof dish – a lasagne dish is ideal. Set the oven at 180°C / 350°F / gas 4. Drain the beans. Put them in a saucepan with fresh water to cover. Bring to the boil, boil vigorously for 45 minutes, then lower the heat, add more boiling water if necessary, cover the pan and simmer for 1-2 hours until tender. Top up the water as necessary. Drain the beans and put them in a mixing bowl with the onions, green pepper, carrot and celery. Warm the molasses in a small saucepan and pour it over the bean mixture. Stir in the herbs, with salt and pepper to taste. Mix in the canned tomatoes.

Spoon the mixture into the prepared dish. Mix the oatmeal, cheese and chives. Spoon the oatmeal mixture over the beans, then drizzle the olive oil over the top. Cover the dish with foil or a lid and bake for 45 minutes. Remove the lid and bake for a further 15 minutes. Serve hot, from the dish.

SERVES 6

NUTRITION NOTE

Soya beans are an excellent source of protein, equivalent in value to that obtained from animal proteins, such as fish, poultry and meat. Soya bean products, such as tofu or bean curd, also provide similar food value.

Three-Bean Sauté

A quick and easy dish for a light meal, this sauté tastes delicious
when served on a base of mixed green salad – crunchy Iceberg
lettuce, some thinly sliced green pepper and sliced cucumber.

FOOD VALUES	TOTAL	PER PORTION
Protein	39g	10g
Carbohydrate	112g	23g
Fat	36g	9g
Fibre	37g	9g
kcals	893	223

100 g / 4 oz shelled broad
  beans
juice of 2 oranges
2 carrots, cut into
  matchstick strips
225 g / 8 oz fine French
  beans
salt and pepper
30 ml / 2 tbsp oil
1 onion, halved and thinly
  sliced
2 (425 g / 15 oz) cans
  butter beans, drained
30 ml / 2 tbsp chopped
  parsley
4 tomatoes, peeled, seeded
  and cut into eighths

Place the broad beans in a saucepan with the
orange juice. Add just enough water to cover the
beans, then bring to the boil. Lower the heat
slightly so that the beans simmer steadily. Cook for
5 minutes.

Add the carrots and French beans, mix well and
sprinkle in a little salt and pepper. Continue to
cook, stirring often, until the carrots are just tender
and the liquid has evaporated to leave the
vegetables juicy. Set aside.

Heat the oil in a clean saucepan and cook the onion
until softened but not browned – about 10 minutes.
Stir in the butter beans and parsley, and cook for 5
minutes, stirring until the beans are hot. Tip the
carrot mixture into the pan, add the tomatoes and
mix well. Cook for 1-2 minutes before serving.

SERVES 4

LIGHT MEALS

Artichokes au Gratin

FOOD VALUES	TOTAL	PER PORTION
Protein	56g	14g
Carbohydrate	89g	22g
Fat	84g	21g
Fibre	2g	1g
kcals	1309	327

675 g / 1½ lb Jerusalem
  artichokes
50 g / 2 oz Cheddar cheese,
  grated
25 g / 1 oz fresh white
  breadcrumbs

CHEESE SAUCE
40 g / 1½ oz butter
40 g / 1½ oz plain flour
450 ml / ¾ pint milk
salt and pepper
40 g / 1½ oz Cheddar
  cheese, grated

Peel the artichokes (see page 20) and cook them in a saucepan of boiling water for 10-15 minutes until tender.

Meanwhile, make the sauce. Melt the butter in a saucepan. Stir in the flour and cook over low heat for 2-3 minutes, without allowing the mixture to colour. Gradually add the milk, stirring constantly until the mixture boils and thickens. Stir in salt and pepper to taste, then add the grated cheese.

Drain the artichokes, tip them into a flameproof dish and pour the cheese sauce over the top. Mix lightly. Combine the cheese and breadcrumbs in a small bowl, sprinkle the mixture over the artichokes and place under a moderate grill until golden brown. Alternatively, brown the topping in a preheated 220°C / 425°F / gas 7 oven for about 10 minutes.

SERVES 4

Cauliflower Cheese

FOOD VALUES	TOTAL	PER PORTION
Protein	94g	24g
Carbohydrate	107g	27g
Fat	129g	32g
Fibre	12g	3g
kcals	1938	485

salt and pepper
1 firm cauliflower
25 g / 1 oz butter
25 g / 1 oz plain flour
200 ml / 7 fl oz milk
125 g / 4½ oz Cheddar
  cheese, grated
pinch of dry mustard
pinch of cayenne pepper
25 g / 1 oz dried white
  breadcrumbs

Bring a saucepan of salted water to the boil, add the cauliflower, cover the pan and cook gently for 15-20 minutes until tender. Drain well, reserving 175 ml / 6 fl oz of the cooking water. Leave the cauliflower head whole or cut carefully into florets. Place in a warmed ovenproof dish, cover with greased greaseproof paper and keep hot.

Set the oven at 220°C / 425°F / gas 7 or preheat the grill. Melt the butter in a saucepan, stir in the flour and cook for 1 minute. Gradually add the milk and reserved cooking water, stirring all the time until the sauce boils and thickens. Remove from the heat and stir in 100 g / 4 oz of the cheese, stirring until it melts into the sauce. Add the mustard and cayenne, with salt and pepper to taste.

Pour the sauce over the cauliflower. Mix the remaining cheese with the breadcrumbs and sprinkle them on top. Brown the topping for 7-10 minutes in the oven or under the grill. Serve.

SERVES 4

VARIATIONS

A wide variety of vegetables can be cooked in this way. Try broccoli (particularly good with grilled bacon); small whole onions; celery, celeriac; leeks or chicory (both taste delicious if wrapped in ham before being covered in the cheese sauce) and asparagus.

Parsnip Soufflé

FOOD VALUES	TOTAL	PER PORTION
Protein	46g	12g
Carbohydrate	72g	18g
Fat	104g	26g
Fibre	11g	3g
kcals	1390	348

butter for greasing
200 g / 7 oz parsnips
salt and pepper
65 g / 2½ oz butter
30 ml / 2 tbsp grated onion
45 ml / 3 tbsp plain flour
100 ml / 3½ fl oz milk
*30 ml / 2 tbsp chopped
  parsley*
pinch of grated nutmeg
4 eggs, separated
*125 ml / 4 fl oz Béchamel
  Sauce (page 94)*

Grease a 1 litre / 1¾ pint soufflé dish. Cook the parsnips in a saucepan with a little boiling salted water for 20-30 minutes until tender. Drain the parsnips, reserving 100 ml / 3½ fl oz of the cooking water, then mash and sieve them, working to a smooth purée. Measure out 150 g / 5 oz purée, and keep the rest on one side. Melt 15 g / ½ oz of the butter in a frying pan and gently cook the onion until soft. Mix it with the 150 g / 5 oz parsnip purée.

Set the oven at 190°C / 375°F / gas 5. Melt the remaining butter in a saucepan, stir in the flour and cook over low heat for 2-3 minutes, without colouring, stirring all the time. Stir the milk into the reserved parsnip cooking water. Over very low heat, gradually add the liquid to the pan, stirring constantly. Bring to the boil, stirring, then simmer for 1-2 minutes until thickened. Stir in the parsnip purée and onion mixture with the parsley. Add salt, pepper and nutmeg to taste. Cool slightly.

Beat the egg yolks into the mixture one by one. In a clean, grease-free bowl, whisk all the egg whites until stiff. Using a metal spoon, fold into the mixture. Spoon the mixture into the prepared dish. Bake for 25-30 minutes, until risen and set. Meanwhile, mix the remaining parsnip purée with the Béchamel sauce in a small saucepan, and heat gently. Serve with the soufflé.

SERVES 4

Potato Soufflé

FOOD VALUES	TOTAL	PER PORTION
Protein	65g	16g
Carbohydrate	84g	21g
Fat	101g	25g
Fibre	6g	2g
kcals	1490	373

butter for greasing
450 g / 1 lb potatoes
salt and pepper
grated nutmeg
100 g / 4 oz Cheddar cheese,
*   finely grated*
50 g / 2 oz butter
125 ml / 4 fl oz milk
30 ml / 2 tbsp chopped
*   parsley*
3 eggs, separated, plus 1 egg
*   white*

Grease a 1 litre / 1¾ pint soufflé dish. Cook the potatoes in a saucepan of boiling salted water for 20-30 minutes.

Set the oven at 190°C / 375°F / gas 5. Mash the potatoes and rub them through a sieve. Add a generous amount of salt, pepper and nutmeg. Stir in the remaining ingredients except the egg whites. Beat well with a wooden spoon until the mixture is smooth.

In a clean, grease-free bowl, whisk all the egg whites until stiff. Using a metal spoon, stir one spoonful of the whites into the potato mixture to lighten it, then fold in the rest until evenly distributed. Spoon the mixture into the prepared dish.

Bake for 30-35 minutes, until well risen and browned. Serve at once.

SERVES 4

Baked Jacket Potatoes

FOOD VALUES	PER POTATO
Protein	11g
Carbohydrate	87g
Fat	1g
Fibre	7g
kcals	374

4 large, even-sized baking
    potatoes
oil for brushing (optional)
butter, flavoured butter,
    fromage frais or low-fat
    soft cheese to serve

Set the oven at 200°C / 400°F / gas 6. Scrub the potatoes, dry them with absorbent kitchen paper and pierce the skin several times with a skewer. If you like soft jackets, brush the potatoes all over with oil.

Bake the potatoes directly on the oven shelf for 1-1½ hours. Test by pressing gently with the fingers. To serve, cut a cross in the top of each potato with a sharp knife. Squeeze the sides of the potato so that the top opens up. Add a pat of plain or flavoured butter or spoon in fromage frais or soft cheese. Serve at once.

SERVES 4

FILLINGS

Make a meal of baked jacket potatoes by cutting them in half, scooping out the centres and mashing them with selected ingredients. Pile the fillings back into the potato shells and heat through, if necessary, in a 180°C / 350°F / gas 4 oven for about 20 minutes. Alternatively, reheat in the microwave oven or under a moderate grill.

NUTRITION NOTE

The food values for the baked potatoes apply to one 275 g / 10 oz potato, without any butter or filling. The values for fillings apply to the filling only, they do not include the values for the potatoes, and the portions serve four.

POTATO TOPPINGS

Try some of these toppings on split baked potatoes.

Egg and Chive
Mash 4 hard-boiled eggs with 30 ml / 2 tbsp plain yogurt. Add 5 ml / 1 tsp tomato ketchup or tomato purée and 30 ml / 2 tbsp snipped chives.

Sardine Mash a 200 g / 7 oz can sardines in tomato sauce and mix with 50 g / 2 oz diced cucumber. Serve with shredded lettuce.

Chick-pea Mash 100 g / 4 oz drained canned chick-peas. Mix with 1 crushed garlic clove and 30 ml / 2 tbsp plain yogurt. Top with chopped spring onion and sesame seeds.

Broccoli and Asparagus Mix 175 g / 6 oz cooked broccoli and 100 g / 4 oz drained canned asparagus tips. Stir in 150 ml / ¼ pint fromage frais, with salt and pepper to taste.

Cheese and Ham Mash the potato. Grate in 100 g / 4 oz Cheddar cheese, add 50 g / 2 oz chopped ham (use trimmings for economy) and mix with 25 g / 1 oz softened butter. Replace in oven until golden.

FOOD VALUES	TOTAL	PER PORTION
Protein	35g	9g
Carbohydrate	–	–
Fat	57g	14g
Fibre	–	–
kcals	656	164

Kipper Mash the potato with 75 g / 3 oz flaked cooked kipper. Add 1 chopped hard-boiled egg, with salt and pepper to taste. Thin with a little milk, if necessary. Reheat.

FOOD VALUES	TOTAL	PER PORTION
Protein	28g	7g
Carbohydrate	1g	–
Fat	16g	4g
Fibre	–	–
kcals	262	66

Frankfurter Mash the potato with butter. For each potato, add 2 heated chopped frankfurters and 15 ml / 1 tbsp tomato relish. Add chopped parsley.

FOOD VALUES	TOTAL	PER PORTION
Protein	22g	6g
Carbohydrate	13g	2g
Fat	56g	14g
Fibre	–	–
kcals	641	160

Tagliatelle with Borlotti Beans

FOOD VALUES	TOTAL	PER PORTION
Protein	76g	19g
Carbohydrate	344g	86g
Fat	83g	21g
Fibre	41g	10g
kcals	2340	585

350 g / 12 oz tagliatelle
salt and pepper
25 g / 1 oz butter
30 ml / 2 tbsp olive oil
1 garlic clove, crushed
1 onion, chopped
100 g / 4 oz button
   mushrooms, sliced
2 (425 g / 15 oz) cans
   borlotti beans, drained
225 g / 8 oz tomatoes, peeled
   and chopped
5 ml / 1 tsp dried oregano
45 ml / 3 tbsp chopped
   parsley
grated Parmesan cheese, to
   serve

Bring a large saucepan of salted water to the boil and cook the pasta. Allow 3 minutes for fresh pasta or about 12 minutes for the dried type. Drain well and set aside.

Heat the butter, oil and garlic in a large frying pan. Add the onion and fry it over gentle heat, stirring, for about 15 minutes or until softened. Add the mushrooms and cook for 5 minutes before stirring in the beans and tomatoes with the herbs. Add salt and pepper to taste and cook for 10 minutes.

Tip the tagliatelle into the pan and toss it with the bean mixture until piping hot about – 5 minutes. Divide between four large bowls and serve with freshly grated Parmesan cheese.

SERVES 4

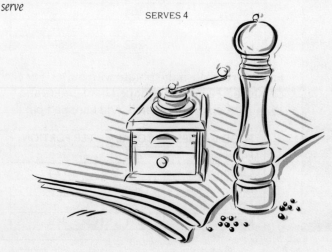

VEGETABLE DRESSINGS FOR PASTA

Vegetables and pasta combine happily to make nutritious light meals. For example, a small amount of cauliflower cheese will delight several hungry adults when served on a base of cooked pasta shapes; and a comparatively small quantity of leftover ratatouille makes a splendid supper dish when tossed with macaroni or spaghetti and served with grated Parmesan cheese.

Aside from the sauced vegetables, simple sautéed mixtures add a pleasing crunch to a plate of tagliatelle. Equally, lightly boiled or steamed broccoli and beans are delicious with pasta shells, the mixture tossed with a little hot olive oil and garlic.

Celery Sauce

Toss pasta shells, rigatoni or macaroni into this creamy sauce.
Serve with freshly ground black pepper and grated Parmesan cheese,
offering a crisp green salad as a refreshing accompaniment.

FOOD VALUES	TOTAL
Protein	20g
Carbohydrate	37g
Fat	23g
Fibre	8g
kcals	420

1 *head of celery, sliced*
300 *ml / ½ pint Chicken Stock or Vegetable Stock (page 44)*
2 *blades of mace*
1 *bay leaf*
25 *g / 1 oz butter*
25 *g / 1 oz plain flour*
salt and pepper
150 *ml / ¼ pint fromage frais*
5-10 *ml / 1-2 tsp lemon juice*

Put the celery in a saucepan with the stock, mace and bay leaf. Simmer for about 20 minutes or until tender, then drain, reserving the celery in a bowl and the stock in a jug.

Melt the butter in a clean pan, add the flour and cook for 1 minute. Gradually add the reserved stock, stirring until the mixture boils and thickens. Add salt and pepper to taste. Remove the sauce from the heat and stir in the celery, with the fromage frais and lemon juice.

MAKES ABOUT 450 ML / ¾ PINT

Béchamel Sauce

FOOD VALUES	TOTAL
Protein	26g
Carbohydrate	71g
Fat	67g
Fibre	2g
kcals	975

1 small onion, thickly sliced
1 small carrot, sliced
1 small celery stick, sliced
600 ml / 1 pint milk
1 bay leaf
few parsley stalks
1 fresh thyme sprig
1 clove
6 white peppercorns
1 blade of mace
salt
50 g / 2 oz butter
50 g / 2 oz plain flour

Combine the onion, carrot, celery and milk in a saucepan. Add the herbs and spices, with salt to taste. Heat to simmering point, cover, turn off the heat and allow to stand for 30 minutes to infuse, then strain.

Melt the butter in a saucepan. Stir in the flour and cook over low heat for 2-3 minutes, without browning. With the heat on the lowest setting, gradually add the flavoured milk, stirring constantly.

Increase the heat to moderate, stirring until the mixture boils and thickens to a coating consistency. Lower the heat when the mixture boils and simmer the sauce for 1-2 minutes, beating briskly to give the sauce a gloss. Add salt if required.

MAKES ABOUT 600 ML / 1 PINT

BECHAMEL SAUCES FOR PASTA

Adapt the basic recipe to make a variety of delicious sauces to serve with pasta. On the right are a few ideas – toss the sauces into plain pasta and offer grated Parmesan cheese at the table.

NUTRITION NOTE

For a less rich sauce, use half white stock and half milk. Semi-skimmed or skimmed milk may be used in place of whole milk to reduce the fat content.

Spinach Sauce Cook, drain and chop 450 g / 1 lb fresh spinach or thaw and drain 225 g / 8 oz frozen chopped spinach. Add the spinach to the sauce, then stir in 30 ml / 2 tbsp snipped chives.

Mushroom Sauce Add 100 g / 4 oz thinly sliced button mushrooms and simmer for 2 minutes.

Broccoli Sauce Cook 225 g / 8 oz fresh broccoli spears in boiling water for 5 minutes, then drain well and roughly chop them. Add to the sauce and season with a little grated nutmeg.

Celery and Spring Onion Sauce Thinly slice 6 celery sticks and chop 4 spring onions. Sweat these vegetables in a small tightly covered saucepan with 15 g / ½ oz butter over gentle heat for 20 minutes, shaking the pan often. Add to the sauce and simmer for 3 minutes before serving.

Fresh Tomato Sauce

FOOD VALUES	TOTAL
Protein	11g
Carbohydrate	39g
Fat	43g
Fibre	10g
kcals	616

30 ml / 2 tbsp olive oil
1 onion, finely chopped
1 garlic clove, crushed
1 bay leaf
1 rindless bacon rasher, chopped
800 g / 1¾ lb tomatoes, peeled and chopped
60 ml / 4 tbsp stock or red wine
salt and pepper
generous pinch of sugar
15 ml / 1 tbsp chopped fresh basil or 5 ml / 1 tsp dried basil

Heat the oil in a saucepan and fry the onion, garlic, bay leaf and bacon over gentle heat for 15 minutes. Stir in the remaining ingredients except the basil. Heat until bubbling, then cover the pan and simmer gently for 30 minutes or until the tomatoes are reduced to a pulp.

Rub the sauce through a sieve into a clean saucepan or purée in a blender or food processor until smooth, then rub through a sieve to remove seeds, if required.

Reheat the sauce. Add the basil. Add more salt and pepper if required before serving.

MAKES ABOUT 600 ML / 1 PINT

Noodles with Mushrooms

FOOD VALUES	TOTAL	PER PORTION
Protein	69g	17g
Carbohydrate	263g	66g
Fat	93g	23g
Fibre	15g	4g
kcals	2101	523

15 g / ½ oz butter
30 ml / 2 tbsp oil
2 rindless streaky bacon
  rashers, chopped
450 g / 1 lb open
  mushrooms, sliced
salt and pepper
350 g / 12 oz noodles
150 ml / ¼ pint fromage
  frais

Melt the butter in the oil in a large frying pan. Add the bacon and fry for 2 minutes, then stir in the mushrooms. Add salt and pepper to taste and cook over moderately high heat, stirring occasionally, for about 10 minutes.

Meanwhile cook the noodles in a large saucepan of boiling salted water for 8-10 minutes or until tender but still firm to the bite.

Stir the fromage frais into the mushrooms and heat briefly over low heat. Drain the noodles thoroughly, pour the mushroom mixture over the top and toss lightly. Serve at once.

SERVES 4

VEGETABLE ACCOMPANIMENTS

Beans with Creamy Dressing

Fromage frais replaces soured cream in this tempting side dish which goes well with simple grilled meats.

FOOD VALUES	TOTAL	PER PORTION (3)
Protein	22g	7g
Carbohydrate	46g	15g
Fat	24g	8g
Fibre	9g	3g
kcals	476	159

fat for greasing
450 g / 1 lb runner beans
150 ml / ¼ pint fromage frais
1.25 ml / ¼ tsp grated nutmeg
1.25 ml / ¼ tsp caraway seeds
salt and pepper
25 g / 1 oz butter
50 g / 2 oz fresh white breadcrumbs

Set the oven at 200°C / 400°F / gas 6. Grease a 1 litre / 1¾ pint baking dish. Wash the beans, string them if necessary and slice them thinly. Cook in boiling water for 3-7 minutes until cooked to taste. Alternatively, cook in a steamer over boiling water. Drain thoroughly.

Combine the fromage frais, nutmeg and caraway seeds in a bowl. Stir in salt and pepper to taste. Add the beans and toss well together. Spoon the mixture into the prepared baking dish.

Melt the butter in a small frying pan, add the breadcrumbs and fry over gentle heat for 2-3 minutes. Sprinkle the mixture over the beans. Bake for 20-30 minutes or until the topping is golden.

SERVES 3 TO 4

MICROWAVE TIP

The first stage of this recipe – cooking the runner beans – may be done in the microwave. Put the beans in a dish with 60 ml / 4 tbsp water. Cover loosely and cook on High for 10-12 minutes, stirring once or twice. Take care when removing the cover to avoid being scalded by the steam.

Broad Beans with Cream Sauce

FOOD VALUES	TOTAL	PER PORTION
Protein	47g	12g
Carbohydrate	61g	15g
Fat	30g	8g
Fibre	29g	7g
kcals	685	171

250 ml / 8 fl oz Chicken
  Stock (page 44)
15 ml / 1 tbsp chopped fresh
  herbs (parsley, thyme,
  sage, savory)
1 kg / 2¼ lb broad beans,
  shelled
1 egg yolk
150 ml / ¼ pint reduced-fat
  single cream
salt and pepper

Combine the stock and herbs in a saucepan.
Bring to the boil, add the beans and cook for
5-15 minutes until tender. Lower the heat to a
bare simmer.

Beat the egg yolk with the cream in a small bowl.
Add 30 ml / 2 tbsp of the hot stock and mix well,
then pour the contents of the bowl into the pan.
Heat gently, stirring all the time, until the sauce
thickens slightly. Do not allow the mixture to boil
or it will curdle. Add salt and pepper to taste
and serve.

SERVES 4

NUTRITION NOTE

To reduce the fat content of this dish when preparing it for an everyday meal,
omit the egg yolk and stir fromage frais into the sauce instead of the cream.
Heat the sauce very gently as fromage frais curdles extremely easily.

Stir-Fried Beans with Savory

FOOD VALUES	TOTAL	PER PORTION
Protein	8g	2g
Carbohydrate	22g	6g
Fat	36g	9g
Fibre	19g	5g
kcals	435	109

450 g / 1 lb French beans,
   trimmed
salt and pepper
15 ml / 1 tbsp butter
15 ml / 1 tbsp oil
15 ml / 1 tbsp finely chopped
   fresh summer savory
4 spring onions, thinly sliced

Cook the beans in boiling salted water for 2 minutes, then drain, refresh under cold running water and drain again.

Melt the butter in the oil in a large frying pan or wok. Add the beans and half the savory. Stir fry for 3 minutes. Add the spring onions, with salt and pepper to taste, and stir fry for 2-3 minutes more. The beans should be tender but still crisp. Sprinkle with the remaining savory and serve at once.

SERVES 4

VARIATION

Use only 225 g / 8 oz beans and add 225 g / 8 oz sliced button mushrooms with the onions. Substitute 10 ml / 2 tsp fennel seeds for the savory, if liked. A few water chestnuts, thinly sliced, may be added for extra crunch.

NUTRITION NOTE

Stir frying is a useful cooking method in a healthy diet for two reasons – firstly, because the food is kept moving all the time, the amount of fat used can be reduced to the minimum; secondly, because the speedy cooking helps to retain the maximum food value of the vegetables.

Polish Beetroot

FOOD VALUES	TOTAL	PER PORTION
Protein	31g	5g
Carbohydrate	106g	18g
Fat	24g	4g
Fibre	15g	3g
kcals	739	123

30 ml / 2 tbsp butter
1 small onion, finely
    chopped
30 ml / 2 tbsp plain flour
250 ml / 8 fl oz plain yogurt
675 g / 1½ lb cooked
    beetroot, peeled and
    grated
30 ml / 2 tbsp finely grated
    horseradish
salt and pepper
sugar (optional)
15 ml / 1 tbsp chopped
    parsley to garnish

Melt the butter in a saucepan, add the onion and fry for 4-6 minutes until soft but not coloured. Stir in the flour and cook for 1 minute, then lower the heat and gradually stir in the yogurt.

Bring to the boil, stirring constantly until the sauce thickens. Add the beetroot and horseradish and heat thoroughly. Season to taste with salt and pepper, and add a little sugar, if liked. Serve hot, garnished with the parsley.

SERVES 6

Bavarian Cabbage

FOOD VALUES	TOTAL	PER PORTION
Protein	21g	4g
Carbohydrate	111g	185g
Fat	23g	4g
Fibre	28g	5g
kcals	756	126

25 g / 1 oz butter
1 onion, finely chopped
1.1 kg / 2½ lb white cabbage, washed, quartered and shredded
1 cooking apple
salt and pepper
10 ml / 2 tsp sugar
125 ml / 4 fl oz Vegetable Stock (page 44) or water
1.25 ml / ¼ tsp caraway seeds
15 ml / 1 tbsp cornflour
60 ml / 4 tbsp white wine

Melt the butter in a heavy-bottomed saucepan. Add the onion and fry gently for 10 minutes until soft but not coloured. Stir in the cabbage, tossing it lightly in the fat.

Peel and core the apple, chop it finely and stir it into the pan. Add salt and pepper to taste, then stir in the sugar, stock or water, and caraway seeds. Cover the pan with a tight-fitting lid and simmer very gently for 1 hour.

Meanwhile mix the cornflour and wine together in a small bowl. Stir the mixture into the pan. Bring to the boil, stirring the mixture constantly until it thickens. Cook for 2-3 minutes, still stirring. Serve.

SERVES 6

VARIATION

For a slightly more fruity flavour, increase the number of apples to 2 and substitute cider for the stock and wine. Omit the caraway seeds.

Sauerkraut with Juniper Berries

One of the oldest forms of preserved food, sauerkraut is simply fermented cabbage. It is sometimes possible to buy it loose from a large barrel in a delicatessen, but is more generally sold in cans or jars.

FOOD VALUES	TOTAL	PER PORTION
Protein	27g	7g
Carbohydrate	39g	10g
Fat	55g	14g
Fibre	12g	3g
kcals	747	187

400 g / 14 oz sauerkraut
15 g / ½ oz butter
4 rindless streaky bacon
  rashers, chopped
1 large onion, chopped
1 garlic clove, crushed
6 juniper berries, crushed
2 bay leaves
5 ml / 1 tsp caraway seeds
250 ml / 8 fl oz Chicken
  Stock (page 44)
salt and pepper (optional)

Put the sauerkraut in a large bowl, add cold water to cover and soak for 15 minutes. Drain thoroughly, then squeeze dry. Melt the butter in a saucepan, add the bacon and onion and fry over gentle heat for about 10 minutes. Add all the remaining ingredients, cover the pan and simmer for 1 hour. Add salt and pepper, if required, before serving.

SERVES 4

MRS BEETON'S TIP

For a richer, creamier flavour, stir in 150 ml / ¼ pint plain yogurt or soured cream just before serving the sauerkraut. Do not allow the mixture to approach boiling point after adding the yogurt or cream.

Carrots with Cider

This traditional way of cooking carrots – by sweating them in a little fat and adding the minimum amount of liquid – was originally known as 'the conservation method' because it preserved as many of the nutrients as possible.

FOOD VALUES	TOTAL	PER PORTION
Protein	7g	1g
Carbohydrate	46g	8g
Fat	32g	5g
Fibre	16g	3g
kcals	521	87

25 g / 1 oz butter
675 g / 1 ½ lb young
   carrots, trimmed and
   scraped
salt
60 ml / 4 tbsp reduced-fat
   single cream
125 ml / 4 fl oz dry cider
few drops of lemon juice
pepper

Melt the butter in a heavy-bottomed saucepan. Add the carrots and cook over very gentle heat for 10 minutes, shaking the pan frequently so that the carrots do not stick to the base. Pour over a little boiling water, with salt to taste. Cover the pan and simmer the carrots for about 10 minutes more or until tender and all the liquid has evaporated.

Gradually stir in the cream and cider. Add the lemon juice and salt and pepper to taste. Cover the pan and cook gently for 10 minutes more. Serve.

SERVES 6

MRS BEETON'S TIP

Another way of preserving as many nutrients as possible is to cook the carrots in the microwave, but the results will be more satisfactory if smaller quantities are used. Combine 225 g / 8 oz young carrots with 30 ml / 2 tbsp butter in a dish. Cover loosely and cook on High for 5-7 minutes, stirring once. Before serving, add salt and pepper to taste.

Cauliflower with Beans

FOOD VALUES	TOTAL	PER PORTION (4)
Protein	22g	6g
Carbohydrate	27g	7g
Fat	71g	18g
Fibre	14g	4g
kcals	823	206

45 ml / 3 tbsp oil
knob of butter (optional)
1 small onion, chopped
1 small cauliflower, broken
  into florets
225 g / 8 oz French beans,
  trimmed and cut in pieces
  or thawed and drained if
  frozen
salt and pepper
15-45 ml / 1-3 tbsp chopped
  fresh herbs

Heat the oil and butter (if used) in a large frying pan or wok. Stir fry the onion for 5 minutes, until slightly softened. Add the cauliflower and cook, stirring, for 5 minutes, until the florets are translucent and lightly cooked.

Add the beans and continue stir frying for a further 3-4 minutes or until all the vegetables are just cooked but still crunchy. Add salt and pepper to taste and stir in the herbs. Serve.

SERVES 4 TO 6

Courgettes with Dill

FOOD VALUES	TOTAL	PER PORTION
Protein	12g	3g
Carbohydrate	12g	3g
Fat	23g	6g
Fibre	6g	2g
kcals	306	77

25 g / 1 oz butter
grated rind of ½ lemon
8 small courgettes, trimmed
  and sliced
salt and pepper
45 ml / 3 tbsp chopped
  fresh dill
squeeze of lemon juice

Melt the butter in a large frying pan. Add the lemon rind and cook for a few seconds before adding the courgettes. Cook over medium to high heat for 2-3 minutes, then add salt and pepper, and the dill. Toss in a little lemon juice and serve.

SERVES 4

Panfried Onion and Apple

FOOD VALUES	TOTAL	PER PORTION
Protein	6g	2g
Carbohydrate	79g	20g
Fat	34g	9g
Fibre	11g	3g
kcals	620	155

40 g / 1 ½ oz butter
350 g / 12 oz onions, sliced
  in rings
450 g / 1 lb cooking apples
10 ml / 2 tsp caster sugar
salt and pepper

Melt the butter in a heavy-bottomed frying pan. Add the onions and fry gently. Peel, core and slice the apples into the pan. Mix lightly to coat the apples in the melted butter. Sprinkle the sugar over the top, cover and simmer for 30 minutes or until the onions and apples are tender. Add salt and pepper to taste before serving.

SERVES 4

Fennel with Leeks

FOOD VALUES	TOTAL	PER PORTION
Protein	21g	5g
Carbohydrate	34g	9g
Fat	5g	1g
Fibre	31g	8g
kcals	305	76

4 fennel bulbs, trimmed and
  halved
juice of ½ lemon
knob of butter or 30 ml /
  2 tbsp olive oil
4 leeks, sliced
1 bay leaf
2 fresh thyme sprigs
salt and pepper
150 ml / ¼ pint Chicken
  Stock or Vegetable Stock
  (page 44)
45 ml / 3 tbsp dry sherry
  (optional)

Set the oven at 180°C / 350°F / gas 4. As soon as the
fennel has been prepared, sprinkle the lemon juice
over the cut bulbs. Heat the butter or oil in a frying
pan and sauté the leeks for 2 minutes to soften
them slightly. Add the pieces of fennel to the pan,
pushing the leeks to one side. Turn the pieces of
fennel in the fat for a minute or so, then tip the
contents of the pan into an ovenproof casserole.

Add the bay leaf and thyme to the vegetables and
sprinkle in salt and pepper to taste. Pour the stock
and sherry (if used) over the fennel and cover the
dish. Bake for 1-1¼ hours, turning the fennel
mixture over twice, until tender. Taste for
seasoning, remove the bay leaf and serve.

SERVES 4

Lettuce with Herb Sauce

FOOD VALUES	TOTAL	PER PORTION
Protein	10g	2g
Carbohydrate	26g	4g
Fat	24g	4g
Fibre	6g	1g
kcals	346	58

salt and pepper
6 small heads of lettuce,
   trimmed
25 g / 1 oz butter
25 g / 1 oz plain flour
250 ml / 8 fl oz Chicken
   Stock or Vegetable Stock
   (page 44)
10 ml / 2 tsp snipped chives
1 bay leaf
10 ml / 2 tsp chopped
   parsley

Bring a large saucepan of salted water to the boil, add the lettuces and blanch for 2 minutes. Drain thoroughly, blotting excess water with absorbent kitchen paper.

Melt the butter in a small saucepan, stir in the flour and cook for 1 minute. Gradually add the stock, stirring all the time until the mixture boils and thickens. Stir in the herbs, with salt and pepper to taste. Add the lettuces.

Cover the pan and cook the lettuces in the sauce for 20-30 minutes, stirring occasionally, but taking care not to break up the heads. Remove the bay leaf, add more salt and pepper if required, and serve.

SERVES 6

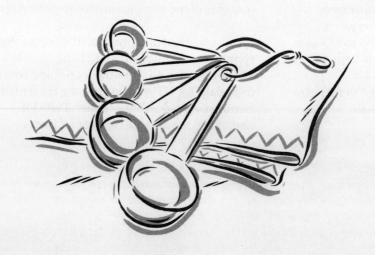

Creamed Onions

FOOD VALUES	TOTAL	PER PORTION (6)
Protein	32g	5g
Carbohydrate	143g	24g
Fat	70g	12g
Fibre	16g	3g
kcals	1297	216

fat for greasing
1 kg / 2¼ lb small onions, peeled but left whole
100 ml / 3½ fl oz reduced-fat single cream
Béchamel sauce (page 94) made using 300 ml / ½ pint milk
grated nutmeg
salt and pepper
50 g / 2 oz dried white breadcrumbs
25 g / 1 oz butter
30 ml / 2 tbsp chopped parsley

Grease a 1 litre / 1¾ pint casserole. Set the oven at 160°C / 325°F / gas 3. Bring a saucepan of water to the boil. Add the onions and cook for 10-15 minutes until just tender. Drain well.

Add the cream to the Béchamel sauce and reheat gently without boiling. Stir in the nutmeg with salt and pepper to taste, add the onions and mix lightly.

Spoon the mixture into the prepared casserole. Top with the breadcrumbs and dot with the butter. Bake for 20 minutes. Serve hot, sprinkled with the parsley.

SERVES 6 TO 8

MRS BEETON'S TIP

To make about 100 g / 4 oz dried breadcrumbs, cut the crusts off six slices (175 g / 6 oz) of bread, then spread the bread out on baking sheets. Bake in a preheated 150°C / 300°F / gas 2 oven for about 30 minutes until dry but not browned. Cool, then crumb in a food processor or blender. Alternatively, put the dried bread between sheets of greaseproof paper; crush with a rolling pin.

Onions and Tomatoes in Cider

FOOD VALUES	TOTAL	PER PORTION (6)
Protein	13g	2g
Carbohydrate	66g	11g
Fat	43g	7g
Fibre	12g	2g
kcals	723	121

6 large onions, peeled but
left whole
50 g / 2 oz butter or
margarine
225 g / 8 oz tomatoes, peeled
and sliced
2 bay leaves
2 cloves
150 ml / ¼ pint medium
cider
125 ml / 4 fl oz Vegetable
Stock (page 44)
salt and pepper

Bring a saucepan of water to the boil. Add the
onions and cook for 2 minutes, then drain
thoroughly. Cool, cut into rings and dry on
absorbent kitchen paper.

Melt the butter or margarine in a deep frying pan.
Add the onion rings. Fry over gentle heat until
golden. Add the tomatoes, bay leaves, cloves, cider
and stock. Cover and simmer for 45 minutes.
Remove the bay leaves and cloves, season and
serve at once.

SERVES 6

Onions Italian-Style

FOOD VALUES	TOTAL	PER PORTION
Protein	8g	1g
Carbohydrate	64g	11g
Fat	31g	5g
Fibre	9g	2g
kcals	553	92

675 g / 1½ lb button onions
30 ml / 2 tbsp olive oil
2 bay leaves
2 cloves
4 white peppercorns
30 ml / 2 tbsp white wine
   vinegar
5 ml / 1 tsp caster sugar

Cook the onions in their skins in a saucepan of boiling water for 15-20 minutes, until just tender. Drain. When cool enough to handle, slip off the skins.

Heat the oil in a saucepan. Put in the bay leaves, cloves and peppercorns and shake the pan over moderate heat for 2-3 minutes. Add the onions to the pan and cook very gently for 5 minutes. Stir in the vinegar and sugar. Continue cooking until the liquid is reduced to a syrup. Serve hot.

SERVES 6

MRS BEETON'S TIP

Try to find silverskin or small white onions for this recipe. Slices of the deep reddish-purple Italian onions may also be used, in which case substitute red wine vinegar for the white.

Sweet Parsnip Bake

FOOD VALUES	TOTAL	PER PORTION
Protein	16g	3g
Carbohydrate	200g	33g
Fat	27g	5g
Fibre	27g	5g
kcals	1060	177

fat for greasing
450 g / 1 lb parsnips, sliced
250 ml / 8 fl oz apple purée
75 g / 3 oz soft light brown
  sugar
salt
2.5 ml / ½ tsp grated
  nutmeg
15 ml / 1 tbsp lemon juice
75 g / 3 oz fresh
  breadcrumbs
25 g / 1 oz butter, diced
1.25 ml / ¼ tsp paprika

Grease an ovenproof dish. Set the oven at 190°C / 375°F / gas 5. Put the parsnips in a saucepan of cold water, bring to the boil and cook for 15-20 minutes or until tender. Drain thoroughly, then mash the parsnips by hand or purée in a blender or food processor.

Arrange alternate layers of parsnip purée and apple purée in the prepared dish, sprinkling each layer with brown sugar, salt, nutmeg and lemon juice. Top with the breadcrumbs, butter and a dusting of paprika. Bake for 30 minutes.

SERVES 6

MRS BEETON'S TIP

Horseradish sauce or creamed horseradish make interesting condiments for parsnips. Beat a couple of spoonfuls into mashed, boiled parsnips, adding a knob of butter. Taste as you add, and remember that horseradish sauce is far hotter than creamed horseradish.

Pease Pudding

FOOD VALUES	TOTAL	PER PORTION
Protein	153g	26g
Carbohydrate	332g	55g
Fat	41g	7g
Fibre	30g	5g
kcals	2225	371

575 g / 1¼ lb split peas, soaked overnight in cold water to cover
1 small onion, peeled but left whole
1 bouquet garni
salt and pepper
25 g / 1 oz butter, cut into small pieces
2 eggs, beaten

Drain the peas, put them in a saucepan and add cold water to cover. Add the onion, the bouquet garni and salt and pepper to taste. Bring to the boil, skim off any scum on the surface of the liquid, then reduce the heat to very low and simmer the peas for 2-2½ hours or until tender.

Drain the peas thoroughly. Press them through a sieve or purée in a blender or food processor. Add the pieces of butter with the beaten eggs. Beat well.

Spoon the mixture into a floured pudding cloth and tie tightly. Suspend the bag in a large saucepan of boiling salted water and simmer gently for 1 hour. Remove from the pan, take the pudding out of the cloth and serve very hot.

SERVES 6

MRS BEETON'S TIP

Modern cooks, unfamiliar with pudding cloths, can bake this nutritious pudding in a greased casserole. It will need about 30 minutes to cook in a preheated 180°C / 350°F / gas 4 oven.

COOKING VEGETABLES
IN THE MICROWAVE

Preparation

With the exception of frozen produce, the majority of vegetables should have a small amount of water added before cooking. Prepare the vegetables as usual, following the instructions in the general guide on pages 20 to 40 if in any doubt, then place them in a covered container with a little water. Do not add any salt.

In some cases a knob of butter may be added instead of water, for example with courgettes (which are naturally moist), or wine or citrus juice may be used with or without a little butter.

When cooking large whole potatoes, arrange them as far apart as possible on a large plate, dish or double-thick absorbent kitchen paper. Remember to prick potatoes before cooking them so that they do not burst.

Arrange cauliflower and broccoli so that the tender heads are close together in the middle of the dish. The stalks, which are tougher and denser, should be spaced around the rim of the dish so that they receive the maximum microwave energy. This principle should be applied to all vegetables in which some parts are more tender than others. When cooking florets in a deep dish, arrange them with the stalks pointing outwards and upwards so that the tender heads are together in the middle.

Quantities

Microwave cooking is excellent for small to medium quantities of vegetables; however large quantities are best split into two batches for cooking.

Cooking Notes

Stir or rearrange vegetables once or twice during cooking, bringing small pieces from the outside towards the middle. The following times and notes are for cooking on High.

COOKING TIMES

Artichokes, Globe

1	6 – 8 minutes
2	9 – 11 minutes
3	12 – 14 minutes
4	15 – 18 minutes

Size and age affects cooking time. Leave the cooked vegetables to stand, still in their cooking container, for about 5 minutes, after cooking. To test that they are tender, pull off one of the outer leaves – it should come away easily.

Asparagus

Frozen asparagus does not take much longer than fresh but do not add water. Older spears which may be tough are best boiled.

225 g / 8 oz	4 – 6 minutes
450 g / 1 lb	7 – 9 minutes

Beans

Broad Beans

100 g / 4 oz shelled fresh	3 – 4 minutes
225 g / 8 oz shelled fresh	6 – 7 minutes
450 g / 1 lb shelled fresh	9 – 10 minutes
100 g / 4 oz frozen	4 – 5 minutes
225 g / 8 oz frozen	7 – 8 minutes
450 g / 1 lb frozen	11 – 12 minutes

French Beans

100 g / 4 oz fresh	3 – 4 minutes
225 g / 8 oz fresh	5 – 7 minutes
450 g / 1 lb fresh	7 – 10 minutes
100 g / 4 oz frozen	4 – 5 minutes
225 g / 8 oz frozen	7 – 9 minutes
450 g / 1 lb frozen	12 – 14 minutes

Runner Beans

100 g / 4 oz fresh	2 – 3 minutes
225 g / 8 oz fresh	4 – 5 minutes
450 g / 1 lb fresh	6 – 7 minutes
100 g / 4 oz frozen	3 – 6 minutes
225 g / 8 oz frozen	6 – 8 minutes
450 g / 1 lb frozen	8 – 10 minutes

Note Home-frozen runner beans that are in a block should be broken as they thaw. They take longer to thaw and cook than purchased frozen beans.

Broccoli

100 g / 4 oz fresh	2 – 4 minutes
225 g / 8 oz fresh	5 – 6 minutes
450 g / 1 lb fresh	7 – 9 minutes
225 g / 8 oz frozen	7 – 8 minutes
450 g / 1 lb frozen	12 – 14 minutes

Leave for 2 minutes before draining and serving.

Brussels Sprouts

100 g / 4 oz fresh	2 – 3 minutes
225 g / 8 oz fresh	4 – 6 minutes
450 g / 1 lb fresh	8 – 10 minutes
100 g / 4 oz frozen	3 – 5 minutes
225 g / 8 oz frozen	7 – 8 minutes
450 g / 1 lb frozen	11 – 12 minutes

Cabbage

Timing depends on personal taste. The following guide gives crunchy results:

100 g / 4 oz	3 – 5 minutes
225 g / 8 oz	6 – 8 minutes
450 g / 1 lb	9 – 11 minutes

Carrots

100 g / 4 oz	2 – 3 minutes
225 g / 8 oz	4 – 5 minutes
450 g / 1 lb	6 – 8 minutes

Note Frozen carrots need very little cooking once they have thawed so follow the above timings but do not add water.

Cauliflower

small whole cauliflower	10 – 12 minutes
large whole cauliflower	13 – 16 minutes
100 g / 4 oz florets	4 – 5 minutes
225 g / 8 oz florets	6 – 8 minutes
450 g / 1 lb florets	10 – 12 minutes

Note Frozen florets need very little cooking once they have thawed, so follow the above timings but do not add extra water. For best results, florets should be even in size and not too large.

Corn-on-the-cob

1 fresh	3 – 5 minutes
2 fresh	6 – 8 minutes
3 fresh	8 – 10 minutes
4 fresh	11 – 12 minutes
1 frozen	5 – 7 minutes
2 frozen	8 – 10 minutes
3 frozen	12 – 14 minutes
4 frozen	15 – 17 minutes

Note Do not add water to frozen corn.

Courgettes

225 g / 8 oz	2 – 4 minutes
450 g / 1 lb	4 – 6 minutes

Note Courgettes should be evenly sliced or cut in neat sticks. They cook well in a loosely closed roasting bag.

Leeks

225 g / 8 oz fresh sliced	4 – 6 minutes
450 g / 1 lb fresh sliced	8 – 10 minutes
450 g / 1 lb fresh whole	6 – 8 minutes
225 g / 8 oz frozen sliced	5 – 7 minutes
450 g / 1 lb frozen sliced	10 – 12 minutes

Note Do not add water to frozen leeks.

Marrow

The times are for the prepared vegetable, cut into 2.5-5 cm / 1-2 inch cubes.

225 g / 8 oz	3 – 5 minutes
450 g / 1 lb	7 – 10 minutes

Parsnips

The following times are for prepared vegetables cut into chunks.

450 g / 1 lb	7 – 10 minutes
675 g / 1½ lb	12 – 15 minutes

Leave to stand, still covered, for 3 minutes, then drain. Mash the parsnips or toss them in butter.

Peas

Frozen peas do not require liquid; canned peas should be heated in the can liquid.

225 g / 8 oz fresh	4 – 6 minutes
450 g / 1 lb fresh	7 – 10 minutes
50 g / 2 oz frozen	2 – 3 minutes
100 g / 4 oz frozen	3 – 4 minutes
225 g / 8 oz frozen	4 – 6 minutes
350 g / 12 oz frozen	5 – 7 minutes
450 g / 1 lb frozen	7 – 10 minutes
Small can (about 283 g / 10½ oz)	2 minutes
Large can (about 425 g / 12½ oz)	3 – 4 minutes

Potatoes

Whole Potatoes

The following times are for potatoes weighing about 350 g / 12 oz each, cooked on High.

1	6 – 8 minutes
2	10 – 12 minutes
3	14 – 16 minutes
4	20 – 22 minutes

Old Potatoes

Cut potatoes into large chunks, dice or slice; it is important to make sure the pieces of potato are fairly even in size. Place in a dish and add 45 ml / 3 tbsp water. Do not add salt. Cover and cook on High, rearranging once or twice.

450 g / 1 lb	6 – 8 minutes
675 g / 1½ lb	7 – 10 minutes
1 kg / 2¼ lb	12 – 14 minutes

New Potatoes

Select even-sized new potatoes. Scrub, then place in a dish with 45 ml / 3 tbsp water. Do not add salt. Cover and cook on High, rearranging once or twice.

450 g / 1 lb	5 – 7 minutes
675 g / 1½ lb	6 – 9 minutes
1 kg / 2¼ lb	8 – 11 minutes

Note Small new potatoes take slightly less time than evenly cut old potatoes.

Spinach

Place the trimmed, wet leaves in a bowl or large roasting bag. Cover or close the opening with a microwave-proof tie. Cook on High, rearranging halfway through cooking. Allow 5-7 minutes per 450 g / 1 lb on High. Drain well and use as required.

Sweetcorn

100 g / 4 oz frozen	2 – 4 minutes
225 g / 8 oz frozen	4 – 6 minutes
350 g / 12 oz frozen	6 – 7 minutes
450 g / 1 lb frozen	7 – 10 minutes

Marrow with Tomatoes

FOOD VALUES	TOTAL	PER PORTION
Protein	13g	2g
Carbohydrate	55g	9g
Fat	35g	6g
Fibre	13g	2g
kcals	572	95

30 ml / 2 tbsp olive or
  sunflower oil
1 onion, finely chopped
1-2 garlic cloves, crushed
450 g / 1 lb ripe tomatoes,
  peeled and chopped
10 ml / 2 tsp paprika
15 ml / 1 tbsp tomato purée
1 (1 kg / 2¼ lb) marrow,
  peeled, seeded and cubed
salt and pepper
45 ml / 3 tbsp chopped
  parsley

Heat the oil in a flameproof casserole. Add the onion and garlic, and fry gently for about 15 minutes until soft but not coloured. Stir in the tomatoes, paprika and tomato purée and cook, stirring occasionally, for 10 minutes.

Add the marrow cubes, with salt and pepper to taste. Stir well until simmering, then cover and cook gently for about 25 minutes, stirring occasionally, until tender but not watery. Add the parsley and taste for seasoning.

SERVES 6

VARIATION

Marrow Montgomery Set the oven at 190°C / 375°F / gas 5. Add the marrow as above, then stir in 40 g / 1½ oz cubed dark rye bread. Buy an unsliced rye loaf for this recipe as the pre-sliced bread sold in packets is cut too thin. Bake the mixture, uncovered, for 30-40 minutes, sprinkle with parsley and serve.

Potatoes Lyonnaise

This is a very good way of using up leftover boiled new potatoes.
A crushed garlic clove may be added to the onion, if liked.

FOOD VALUES	TOTAL	PER PORTION
Protein	24g	4g
Carbohydrate	190g	32g
Fat	35g	6g
Fibre	16g	3g
kcals	1126	188

1 kg / 2¼ lb potatoes,
scrubbed but not peeled
40 g / 1½ oz butter or
margarine
225 g / 8 oz onions, thickly
sliced
salt and pepper
15 ml / 1 tbsp chopped
parsley

Boil or steam the potatoes in their jackets until tender. When cool enough to handle, peel and cut into slices 5 mm / ¼ inch thick.

Melt the butter or margarine in a large frying pan. Add the onions and fry over moderate heat until just golden. Using a slotted spoon, transfer the onions to a plate; keep warm. Add the potatoes to the fat remaining in the pan and fry on both sides until crisp and golden.

Return the onions to the pan and mix with the potatoes. Add salt and pepper to taste, turn into a serving dish and sprinkle with the parsley.

SERVES 6

MRS BEETON'S TIP

Use an electric frying pan, if you have one, for this recipe. The size and depth means that the onions and potatoes will be easy to cook, and the readily-controlled temperature will be an asset when frying the potatoes.

SALADS

SALADS IN A HEALTHY DIET

The British attitude to salad has changed enormously over the past century or more. In Mrs Beeton's day, the dish was likely to consist of the few raw vegetables that were cultivated in summer and cold cooked root vegetables in winter. Raw vegetables were considered to be indigestible and unsuitable for consumption in quantity, certainly not for anyone of a delicate digestive disposition. Although lettuce was used for dainty luncheon dishes, cooked vegetables, such as potatoes, celery, beans and potatoes, were preferred.

Today an excellent choice of salad leaves and vegetables is available in most supermarkets throughout the year. Recipes are more adventurous than ever before; salads are interesting and satisfying to eat and they play an essential role in a healthy, balanced diet. The value of eating raw fruit and vegetables is widely recognised not only for the fibre they contribute to the diet but also for the vitamin content which is so easily reduced or destroyed by cooking.

Increasing the number of salads eaten on a regular basis is a matter of habit, starting with the shopping routine. Try to buy salad vegetables more often – two or three times a week, depending on the time of year and your household size. If there are just one or two people in the family, it is sensible to select ingredients which keep well, such as Chinese leaves, Iceberg lettuce, celery, carrots, cucumber, peppers and tomatoes, as main salad ingredients. Unless you can use them promptly, avoid buying the softer-leafed lettuces which have to be eaten within a day of purchase for maximum flavour. Remember that salads do not have to be restricted to formal meals – pack sandwiches with salad ingredients, fill bread rolls, chunks of French bread or pitta bread with salad, include a sealed container of salad as part of a packed lunch and eat pieces of raw vegetable and fruit as a snack.

TOSSING AN EXCELLENT SALAD

- Ingredients – both raw and cooked – must be fresh and in prime condition.
- Select ingredients which complement each other in terms of flavour and texture.
- Do not use so many ingredients that the salad ends up as a kaleidoscope of unrecognizable, clashing flavours.
- Ingredients such as cut beetroot, which discolour or shed colour, should be prepared and added just before serving.
- Salads, salad leaves and greens which rapidly become limp should be dressed at the last minute.

SIDE SALADS

If the salad is to accompany a main food, for example as a garnish for a starter or to support a main course dish, choose ingredients and a dressing which

complement the main food. Side salads should be simple, with clearly defined flavours and a light dressing.

Plain Green Salad Do not underestimate the value of a good, crisp, really fresh lettuce lightly tossed with a well-seasoned, oil-based dressing. This makes an ideal accompaniment for grilled fish, meat or poultry, or may be served with the cheese course. This classic green salad counteracts the richness of the main dish and refreshes the palate.

Mixed Green Salad This should consist of green ingredients, for example salad leaves, cucumber, green pepper, celery, spring onions, watercress, mustard and cress, and avocado. These flavours go together well; a mixed green salad is ideal for serving with foods such as a quiche, with baked potatoes (topped with low-fat soft cheese, butter, soured cream or fromage frais) and with cold roast meats or grilled pork sausages.

Mixed Salad This type of side salad usually consists of a base of leaves, with other green ingredients, topped with raw items, such as tomatoes, radishes and red or yellow peppers. A mixed salad goes well with cold meats and poultry, cheese or eggs. The ingredients should complement the main dish – grated carrots, shredded cabbage and beetroot may replace some of the other basic ingredients.

Satisfying Side Salads Pasta, rice, beans, grains and potatoes all make good salads, and do not have to be mixed with a cornucopia of ingredients. They should be perfectly cooked, then tossed with selected herbs, such as parsley, mint, basil or tarragon. Additional ingredients should be kept to the minimum: chopped spring onions, diced tomato, and / or chopped olives perhaps. In keeping with the main dish, mayonnaise, yogurt, fromage frais, soured cream or an oil-based mixture may be used to dress the salad.

MAIN COURSE SALADS

Fish and seafood, poultry, meat, game and dairy produce all make excellent salads. Beans and pulses are also suitable. The main food should feature in the same way as for a hot dish, with supporting ingredients and a full-flavoured dressing. It should stand out clearly as the star of the salad, without competition from other ingredients. The salad may be served on a base of shredded lettuce or other salad leaves and a garnish of herbs, nuts or croûtons of toasted or fried bread may be included to balance the texture where necessary. Main course salads often have very plain accompaniments – chunks of crusty French bread or thickly sliced Granary bread (or a baked potato for larger appetites) are usually all that is required.

DRESSINGS

The salad dressing should moisten, blend and develop the flavour of the main ingredients. It should not dominate the dish in any way.

Light Salad Dressings

Many traditional salad dressings have a high fat content which can turn a healthy salad into a rich dish – mayonnaise and soured cream are two classic examples. Although there is a choice of commercial reduced-fat dressings, the following are simple alternatives which give a good flavour.

Yogurt and Chive Dressing Mix 30 ml / 2 tbsp snipped chives with 150 ml / ¼ pint plain yogurt. Stir in 45 ml / 3 tbsp fromage frais and salt and pepper to taste. The fromage frais balances the tang of the yogurt.

Vinaigrette Dressing

FOOD VALUES	TOTAL
Protein	–
Carbohydrate	–
Fat	90g
Fibre	–
kcals	810

90 ml / 6 tbsp light olive oil
salt and pepper
pinch of mustard powder
pinch of caster sugar
30 ml / 2 tbsp white wine
  vinegar
10 ml / 2 tsp finely chopped
  gherkin
5 ml / 1 tsp finely chopped
  onion or chives
5 ml / 1 tsp finely chopped
  parsley
5 ml / 1 tsp finely chopped
  capers
5 ml / 1 tsp finely chopped
  fresh tarragon or chervil

Mix all the ingredients in a screw-topped jar. Close the jar tightly and shake vigorously until well blended; then allow to stand for at least 1 hour. Shake again before using.

MAKES ABOUT 125 ML / 4 FL OZ

Aurore Dressing Peel, seed and finely chop 4 tomatoes, then mix them with 1 finely chopped spring onion, 2.5 ml / ½ tsp caster sugar, 5 ml / 1 tsp tomato purée and salt and pepper. Stir the tomato mixture into 250 ml / 8 fl oz fromage frais.

Orange and Walnut Dressing Mix a little salt and pepper with the freshly squeezed juice of 2 oranges. Add 30 ml / 2 tbsp finely chopped parsley and 15 ml / 1 tbsp finely chopped onion. Whisk in 15 ml / 1 tbsp walnut oil.

Lemon and Soy Sauce Dressing Whisk 2.5 ml / ½ tsp grated lemon rind, the juice of 1 lemon, 15 ml / 1 tbsp light soy sauce and a little caster sugar to taste together. This dressing has a strong flavour.

Chiffonade Dressing

FOOD VALUES	TOTAL
Protein	16g
Carbohydrate	3g
Fat	98g
Fibre	1g
kcals	958

2 *hard-boiled eggs, finely chopped*
½ *small red pepper, seeded and finely chopped*
30 ml / 2 tbsp *finely chopped parsley*
5 ml / 1 tsp *very finely chopped shallot*
125 ml / 4 fl oz *Vinaigrette Dressing (left)*

Combine all the ingredients in a small bowl. Whisk with a balloon whisk to blend thoroughly.

MAKES 150 ML / ¼ PINT

French Bean and Tomato Salad

FOOD VALUES	TOTAL	PER PORTION
Protein	6g	2g
Carbohydrate	14g	4g
Fat	47g	12g
Fibre	7g	2g
kcals	498	125

salt and pepper
225 g / 8 oz French beans,
    trimmed
3 tomatoes, peeled, seeded
    and quartered
15 ml / 1 tbsp snipped chives

DRESSING
45 ml / 3 tbsp walnut or
    sunflower oil
10 ml / 2 tsp white wine
    vinegar
5 ml / 1 tsp lemon juice
pinch of caster sugar
pinch of mustard powder
1 garlic clove, crushed

Make the dressing by mixing all the ingredients in a screw-topped jar. Add salt and pepper to taste, close the jar tightly and shake vigorously until well blended.

Bring a small saucepan of salted water to the boil. Add the beans and cook for 5-10 minutes or until just tender. Drain, rinse briefly under cold water, drain again, then tip into a bowl. Immediately add the dressing and toss the beans in it. Leave to cool.

Add the tomatoes and toss lightly. Taste the salad and add more salt and pepper if required. Turn into a salad bowl, sprinkle with the chives and serve.

SERVES 4

MICROWAVE TIP

Wash the beans. Drain lightly, leaving some moisture on the pods. Place them in a roasting bag, tie the top loosely with an elastic band and microwave on High for 5 minutes. Shake the bag carefully, set it aside for 1 minute, then transfer the contents to a bowl and add the dressing and remaining ingredients. Toss lightly.

Beetroot and Celery Salad

FOOD VALUES	TOTAL	PER PORTION
Protein	9g	2g
Carbohydrate	91g	23g
Fat	84g	21g
Fibre	14g	4g
kcals	1133	283

450 g / 1 lb cooked beetroot
1 celery heart
2 green-skinned eating
　apples
50 g / 2 oz walnuts, roughly
　chopped
15 ml / 1 tbsp chopped
　parsley
watercress to garnish

DRESSING
30 ml / 2 tbsp olive or
　sunflower oil
15 ml / 1 tbsp cider vinegar
pinch of mustard powder
1.25 ml / ¼ tsp soft light
　brown sugar
salt and pepper

Peel the beetroot and cut a few neat rounds for the garnish. Dice the rest neatly. Use one stick of the celery to make curls (see Mrs Beeton's Tip) and chop the rest.

Mix the dressing ingredients together in a screw-topped jar. Close tightly and shake well. Quarter, core and dice the apples and put them in a salad bowl. Add the dressing, tossing the apples in it to prevent discoloration. Add the beetroot, celery, walnuts and parsley. Toss lightly.

Pile the salad into a serving dish and garnish with the reserved beetroot rounds, the celery curls and watercress.

SERVES 6

MRS BEETON'S TIP

The easiest way to make celery curls is to cut the celery stick into 7.5 cm / 3 inch pieces. Make thin slits in each piece, almost to the end, then place in iced water until the ends curl up. Drain well.

Flemish Winter Salad

FOOD VALUES	TOTAL	PER PORTION
Protein	29g	5g
Carbohydrate	110g	18g
Fat	53g	9g
Fibre	12g	2g
kcals	1004	167

450 g / 1 lb cooked potatoes,
  sliced
350 g / 12 oz cooked
  beetroot, sliced
60 ml / 4 tbsp Vinaigrette
  Dressing (page 122)
1 (50 g / 2 oz) can anchovy
  fillets
2 radishes, sliced
dill sprigs to garnish

Layer the potatoes and beetroot in a glass bowl,
sprinkling each layer with a little of the vinaigrette
dressing, and ending with a layer of potatoes.
Arrange a lattice of anchovy fillets on top of the
salad, filling each square with a slice of radish.
Garnish with dill sprigs.

SERVES 6

VARIATION

Reduce the quantities of potatoes and beetroot to
225 g / 8 oz each. Add 1 red-skinned and 1 green-
skinned eating apple, diced but not peeled. Toss
these ingredients with the vinaigrette dressing.

Cabbage Crunch

FOOD VALUES	TOTAL	PER PORTION
Protein	37g	6g
Carbohydrate	62g	10g
Fat	132g	22g
Fibre	23g	4g
kcals	1567	261

100 g / 4 oz white cabbage, shredded
225 g / 8 oz red cabbage, shredded
4 celery sticks, chopped
2 carrots, cut into matchsticks
1 green pepper, seeded and thinly sliced
4 ready-to-eat dried apricots, thinly sliced
100 g / 4 oz pecan nuts or walnuts, chopped
50 g / 2 oz sunflower seeds

DRESSING
1 hard-boiled egg yolk
salt and pepper
1.25 ml / ¼ tsp prepared mustard
dash of Worcestershire sauce
pinch of caster sugar
10 ml / 2 tsp cider vinegar
15 ml / 1 tbsp sunflower oil
30 ml / 2 tbsp double cream

Make the dressing. Sieve the egg yolk into a bowl. Gradually work in the salt and pepper, mustard, Worcestershire sauce, caster sugar and vinegar. Add the oil gradually, beating constantly. Whip the cream in a clean bowl, then fold it into the dressing. Mix all the salad ingredients in a bowl, add the dressing and toss lightly.

SERVES 6

VARIATION

Low-fat Cheese Dressing This is delicious with salads that often have traditional mayonnaise-type or cream-based dressings. Soften 150 g / 5 oz low-fat soft cheese (use the firm, Philadelphia-style cheese) with 30 ml / 2 tbsp skimmed milk, gradually stirring it in to make a smooth dressing. Add salt, pepper and a little prepared mustard to taste. Stir in 15 ml / 1 tbsp snipped chives.

MRS BEETON'S TIP

Remember that full-flavoured, firm-textured salads like this one make excellent fillings for piping-hot baked potatoes. Not only does the flavour of the salad complement potatoes but the textures also marry well.

Mrs Beeton's Winter Salad

Adding milk to an oil and vinegar dressing gives an unusual, slightly creamy mixture. The milk may be omitted, or mayonnaise thinned with single cream, yogurt or milk may be used instead.

FOOD VALUES	TOTAL	PER PORTION
Protein	40g	7g
Carbohydrate	36g	6g
Fat	60g	10g
Fibre	8g	1g
kcals	831	139

1 head of endive, washed and shredded
1 punnet of mustard and cress
2 celery sticks, thinly sliced
4 hard-boiled eggs, sliced
225 g / 8 oz cooked beetroot, sliced

DRESSING
5 ml / 1 tsp French mustard
5 ml / 1 tsp caster sugar
30 ml / 2 tbsp salad oil
30 ml / 2 tbsp milk (optional)
30 ml / 2 tbsp cider vinegar
salt
cayenne pepper

Arrange the endive, mustard and cress and celery in a salad bowl. Top with the eggs and beetroot, overlapping the slices or interleaving them with the endive but keeping them separate from each other.

For the dressing, put the mustard and sugar in a small bowl. Gradually add the oil, whisking all the time. Add the milk very slowly (if using), whisking vigorously to prevent the mixture from curdling. Continue adding the vinegar in the same way – if the ingredients are added too quickly the dressing will curdle. Add salt and a hint of cayenne. Spoon this dressing over the salad just before serving.

SERVES 6

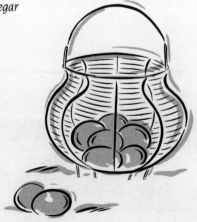

128

Celery and Chestnut Salad

FOOD VALUES	TOTAL	PER PORTION
Protein	9g	2g
Carbohydrate	91g	23g
Fat	84g	21g
Fibre	14g	4g
kcals	1133	283

1 *small lettuce, separated into leaves*
225 *g / 8 oz cooked chestnuts, halved or quartered*
6 *celery sticks, finely chopped*
1 *eating apple*
100 *ml / 3½ fl oz mayonnaise*

Wash the lettuce leaves and dry them thoroughly Line a salad bowl. Put the chestnuts in a bowl with the celery. Peel, core and dice the apple and add it to the bowl with the mayonaise. Mix well. Pile the celery mixture into the lettuce-lined bowl. Serve at once.

SERVES 4

NUTRITION NOTE

To reduce the fat content of the salad, select a reduced-fat mayonnaise or substitute fromage frais, yogurt or low-fat soft cheese for the mayonnaise. Firm textured, low-fat soft cheese may be softened with a little yogurt or milk to make an excellent, creamy dressing (see variation, page 127).

Fennel and Cucumber Salad

FOOD VALUES	TOTAL	PER PORTION
Protein	17g	3g
Carbohydrate	4g	1g
Fat	43g	7g
Fibre	5g	1g
kcals	473	79

½ large cucumber, diced
6 radishes, sliced
1 fennel bulb, sliced
1 garlic clove, crushed
5 ml / 1 tsp chopped mint
2 eggs, hard-boiled and
   quartered, to garnish

DRESSING
30 ml / 2 tbsp olive oil
15 ml / 1 tbsp lemon juice
salt and pepper

Combine the cucumber, radishes, fennel and garlic in a salad bowl. Sprinkle with the mint. Make the dressing by shaking all the ingredients in a tightly-closed screw-topped jar. Pour over the salad, toss lightly and serve with the hard-boiled egg garnish.

SERVES 6

Russian Cucumber Salad

FOOD VALUES	TOTAL	PER PORTION
Protein	52g	13g
Carbohydrate	24g	6g
Fat	27g	7g
Fibre	3g	1g
kcals	543	136

4 hard-boiled egg yolks
250 ml / 8 fl oz fromage frais
few drops of vinegar
1 large cucumber, chilled
salt and pepper
dill sprigs to garnish

Sieve the egg yolks into a bowl, stir in the fromage frais and vinegar and mix well. Chill for 30 minutes. Dice the cucumber, pat it dry with absorbent kitchen paper and place in a dish. Season well, stir in the fromage frais mixture. Garnish and serve.

SERVES 4

Cucumber in Yogurt

FOOD VALUES	TOTAL	PER PORTION (4)
Protein	20g	5g
Carbohydrate	32g	8g
Fat	3g	1g
Fibre	3g	1g
kcals	230	58

1 large cucumber
salt and pepper
300 ml / ½ pint plain
  yogurt, chilled
5 ml / 1 tsp vinegar
  (optional)
30 ml / 2 tbsp chopped mint
pinch of sugar

Cut the cucumber into small dice and place it in a colander. Sprinkle with salt, leave for 3-4 hours, then rinse and drain thoroughly. Pat the cucumber dry on absorbent kitchen paper.

Stir the yogurt, vinegar (if used), mint and sugar together in a bowl. Add the cucumber and mix well. Taste and add salt and pepper if required.

SERVES 4 TO 6

VARIATION

Tsatziki The combination of cucumber and yogurt is an Internationally popular one. This is a Greek-style variation. Grate the cucumber instead of dicing it. Omit the vinegar. The mint is optional but a crushed garlic clove and 15 ml / 1 tbsp finely chopped onion are essential. Mix all the ingredients and serve with warm, fresh bread for a refreshing first course.

MRS BEETON'S TIP

Serve within 1 hour of making, or the liquid in the cucumber may thin the yogurt and spoil the consistency of the salad.

Potato Salad

FOOD VALUES	TOTAL	PER PORTION
Protein	14g	2g
Carbohydrate	146g	24g
Fat	127g	21g
Fibre	9g	2g
kcals	1746	291

salt and pepper
6 large new potatoes or waxy
old potatoes
150 ml / ¼ pint
mayonnaise or Low-fat
Cheese Dressing (see
variation, page 127)
3 spring onions, chopped
30 ml / 2 tbsp chopped
parsley

Bring a saucepan of salted water to the boil, add the potatoes in their jackets and cook for 20-30 minutes until tender. Drain thoroughly. When cool enough to handle, peel and dice the potatoes. Put them in a bowl and add the mayonnaise or dressing while still warm. Lightly stir in the spring onions and parsley, with salt and pepper to taste. Cover, leave to become quite cold and stir before serving.

SERVES 6

VARIATIONS

French Potato Salad Substitute 100 ml / 3½ fl oz Vinaigrette Dressing (page 122) or French dressing for the mayonnaise. Omit the spring onions, increase the parsley to 45 ml / 3 tbsp and add 5 ml / 1 tsp chopped fresh mint and 5 ml / 1 tsp snipped chives.

German Potato Salad Omit the mayonnaise and spring onions. Reduce the parsley to 5 ml / 1 tsp and add 5 ml / 1 tsp finely chopped onion. Heat 60 ml / 4 tbsp Vegetable Stock (page 44) in a saucepan. Beat in 15 ml / 1 tbsp white wine vinegar and 30 ml / 2 tbsp oil. Add salt and pepper to taste. Pour over the diced potatoes while still hot and toss lightly together. Serve at once, or leave to become quite cold.

Potato Salad with Apple and Celery Follow the basic recipe above, but add 2 sliced celery sticks and 1 diced red-skinned apple tossed in a little lemon juice.

Mrs Beeton's Potato Salad

This should be made two or three hours before it is to be served so that the flavours have time to mature. Cold beef, turkey or other poultry may be thinly sliced or cut into chunks and combined with the potato salad to make a light main course dish.

FOOD VALUES	TOTAL	PER PORTION
Protein	8g	1g
Carbohydrate	98g	16g
Fat	92g	15g
Fibre	6g	1g
kcals	1224	204

10 *small cold cooked potatoes*
60 *ml / 4 tbsp tarragon vinegar*
90 *ml / 6 tbsp salad oil*
salt and pepper
15 *ml / 1 tbsp chopped parsley*

Cut the potatoes into 1cm / ½ inch thick slices. For the dressing, mix the tarragon vinegar, oil and plenty of salt and pepper in a screw-topped jar. Close the jar tightly and shake vigorously until well blended.

Layer the potatoes in a salad bowl, sprinkling with a little dressing and the parsley. Pour over any remaining dressing, cover and set aside to marinate before serving.

SERVES 6

VARIATION

Potato and Olive Salad Thinly slice 50 g / 2 oz stoned black olives. Chop 2 spring onions, if liked, and mix them with the olives. Sprinkle the olive mixture between the potato layers.

NUTRITION NOTE

Potatoes make a worthwhile contribution of vitamin C to the traditional British diet. Although they are not a prime source of the vitamin, the frequency of serving and quantity in which they are eaten results in their value. In contemporary diets, where rice and pasta are regularly served instead of potatoes, it is important to recognize the need for serving plenty of vegetables and salads.

Spinach and Bacon Salad

FOOD VALUES	TOTAL	PER PORTION
Protein	42g	11g
Carbohydrate	16g	4g
Fat	121g	30g
Fibre	13g	3g
kcals	1317	329

450 g / 1 lb fresh young spinach
150 g / 5 oz button mushrooms, thinly sliced
1 small onion, thinly sliced
15 ml / 1 tbsp oil
6 rindless bacon rashers, cut into strips
75 ml / 5 tbsp Vinaigrette Dressing (page 122)

Remove the stalks from the spinach, wash the leaves well in cold water, then dry thoroughly on absorbent kitchen paper. If time permits, put the leaves in a polythene bag and chill for 1 hour.

Tear the spinach into large pieces and put into a salad bowl with the mushrooms and onion.

Heat the oil in a small frying pan and fry the bacon until crisp. Meanwhile toss the salad vegetables with the vinaigrette dressing. Drain the hot bacon on absorbent kitchen paper, add to the salad and toss lightly to mix. Serve at once.

SERVES 4

NUTRITION NOTE

If preferred, for a lower-fat salad, the bacon may be grilled until crisp and crumbled into the salad just before serving.

Pepper Salad

FOOD VALUES	TOTAL	PER PORTION (6)
Protein	12g	2g
Carbohydrate	65g	11g
Fat	104g	17g
Fibre	20g	3g
kcals	1227	205

2 *large green peppers*
2 *large red peppers*
2 *large yellow peppers*
1 *mild Italian or Spanish onion, thinly sliced in rings*
100 *ml / 3½ fl oz olive oil*
salt and pepper (optional)

Wash the peppers and pat dry with absorbent kitchen paper. Grill under moderate heat, turning the peppers frequently with tongs until the skins blister, then char all over. Immediately transfer the peppers to a large bowl and cover with several layers of absorbent kitchen paper.

Alternatively, put the grilled peppers in a polythene bag. When cold, rub off the skin under cold water. Remove cores and seeds and cut or tear the peppers into thin strips.

Put the pepper strips on a serving platter, arrange the onion rings around the rim, and drizzle the olive oil over the top. Add salt and pepper to taste, if liked. Serve at once.

SERVES 6 TO 8

NUTRITION NOTE

Peppers are a rich source of vitamin C, especially when fresh and served raw. They are comparatively easy to grow in a greenhouse or conservatory, and their flavour is extremely good when freshly picked.

Tomato Salad

Sun-warmed tomatoes, freshly picked, are perfect for this salad.
In the classic Italian version, olive oil is the only dressing, but a little
red wine vinegar may be added, if preferred.

FOOD VALUES	TOTAL	PER PORTION (4)
Protein	3g	1g
Carbohydrate	14g	4g
Fat	46g	12g
Fibre	5g	1g
kcals	481	120

450 g / 1 lb firm tomatoes,
   peeled and sliced
salt and pepper
pinch of caster sugar
   (optional)
45 ml / 3 tbsp olive oil
5 ml / 1 tsp chopped fresh
   basil
fresh basil sprigs to garnish

Put the tomatoes in a serving dish and sprinkle
lightly with salt and pepper. Add the sugar, if used.
Pour over the olive oil and sprinkle with chopped
basil. Garnish with basil sprigs.

SERVES 4 TO 6

VARIATIONS

Mozzarella and Tomato Salad Interleave the
sliced tomatoes with sliced mozzarella cheese.
Cover and leave to marinate for at least an hour
before serving.

Tomato and Onion Salad A popular salad to serve
with cold meats. Omit the basil. Thinly slice 1 red or
white onion and separate the slices into rings.
Sprinkle these over the tomatoes. Sprinkle with
sugar, salt and pepper, and a few drops of cider
vinegar as well as the oil.

Minted Tomato Salad with Chives Omit the basil.
Sprinkle 15 ml / 1 tbsp chopped fresh mint and 45 ml /
3 tbsp snipped chives over the tomatoes before
adding the oil. Garnish with sprigs of mint.

SWEET SPECIALITIES

Pumpkin Scones

For these delicious scones, use leftover steamed or baked pumpkin cooked without liquid – it will still have to be drained as it is naturally quite watery.

FOOD VALUES	TOTAL	PER SCONE
Protein	39g	3g
Carbohydrate	243g	21g
Fat	31g	3g
Fibre	11g	1g
kcals	1315	109

oil for greasing
300 g / 11 oz well-drained cooked pumpkin
25 g / 1 oz butter, softened
15 ml / 1 tbsp caster sugar
15 ml / 1 tbsp golden syrup or honey
1 egg, beaten
250 g / 9 oz self-raising flour
pinch of salt
2.5 ml / ½ tsp ground cinnamon
1.25 ml / ¼ tsp grated nutmeg

Grease a baking sheet. Set the oven at 230°C / 450°F / gas 8. Mash the pumpkin.

Mix the butter with the sugar and syrup or honey in a bowl. Mix the egg with the pumpkin. Add to the butter and sugar, mixing thoroughly. Sift the flour, salt and spices into a bowl, then fold into the pumpkin mixture to make a soft but not sticky scone dough.

Knead the dough lightly and pat it out to a thickness of 2 cm / ¾ inch. Cut into rounds with a 5 cm / 2 inch cutter. Put the scones on the prepared baking sheet. Bake for 12-15 minutes, until golden brown.

MAKES 12

NUTRITION NOTE

With a low sugar and fat content, scones are a practical choice for an everyday tea-time treat in a healthy diet. Spread them thinly with butter, reserving rich clotted cream and jam toppings for special occasions.

Pumpkin Pie

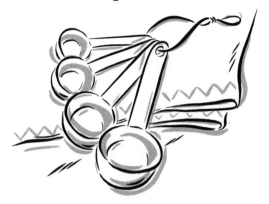

FOOD VALUES	TOTAL	PER PORTION
Protein	56g	9g
Carbohydrate	355g	59g
Fat	116g	19g
Fibre	12g	2g
kcals	2602	434

1 (425 g / 15 oz) can
  pumpkin or 450 g / 1 lb
  cooked mashed pumpkin
150 g / 5 oz soft dark brown
  sugar
7.5 ml / 1½ tsp cinnamon
2.5 ml / ½ tsp salt
5 ml / 1 tsp ground ginger
2.5 ml / ½ tsp grated
  nutmeg
3 eggs
250 ml / 8 fl oz milk

SHORT CRUST PASTRY
225 g / 8 oz plain four
2.5 ml / ½ tsp salt
100 g / 4 oz margarine
flour for rolling out

Set the oven at 200°C / 400°F / gas 6. To make the pastry, sift the flour and salt into a bowl, then rub in the margarine until the mixture resembles fine breadcrumbs. Add enough cold water to make a stiff dough. Press the dough together with your fingertips. Roll out on a lightly floured surface and use to line a 25 cm / 10 inch pie plate. Chill in the refrigerator for 30 minutes.

In a large bowl, mix the pumpkin with the sugar, cinnamon, salt, ginger and nutmeg. Beat the eggs in a second bowl, add the milk and mix well. Stir the egg mixture into the pumpkin mixture. Pour into the pastry case.

Bake for 15 minutes. Lower the temperature to 180°C / 350°F / gas 4 and cook for a further 30-40 minutes, or until a knife inserted in the centre of the pie comes out clean. Cool the pie before serving.

SERVES 6

139

Swiss Carrot Cake

This is more a dessert than a cake. It depends on equal proportions of the main ingredients for its success, so weigh the carrots after grating them.

FOOD VALUES	TOTAL	PER SLICE
Protein	99g	8g
Carbohydrate	348g	29g
Fat	187g	16g
Fibre	28g	2g
kcals	3420	285

oil for greasing
5 eggs, separated
275 g / 10 oz caster sugar
grated rind of ½ lemon
275 g / 10 oz ground
  almonds
275 g / 10 oz grated carrots
2.5 ml / ½ tsp ground
  cinnamon
pinch of ground cloves
45 ml / 3 tbsp plain flour
  and 5 ml / 1 tsp baking
  powder or 45 ml / 3 tbsp
  self-raising flour
pinch of salt
15 ml / 1 tbsp rum, kirsch or
  lemon juice
caster sugar to sprinkle
fromage frais to serve
  (optional)

Grease a shallow 25 cm / 10 inch cake tin or pie dish. Set the oven at 190°C / 375°F / gas 5. Place the egg yolks in a mixing bowl, beat lightly, then add the sugar and beat together until pale and creamy. Stir in the lemon rind and almonds and beat well. Add the grated carrot and stir.

In a bowl, mix the spices, flour and salt and stir into the carrot mixture. Add the rum, kirsch or lemon juice.

In a clean dry bowl, whisk the egg whites until stiff but not dry. Stir 30 ml / 2 tbsp into the carrot mixture, to lighten it, then fold in the rest lightly with a metal spoon. Turn the mixture into the prepared cake tin or pie dish and bake for 1-1½ hours or until a thin hot metal skewer inserted in the centre comes out clean. Cool for a few minutes, then transfer to a wire rack to cool completely.

Sprinkle with caster sugar before serving. Top slices of the cake with fromage frais, if liked.

MAKES ONE 25 CM / 10 INCH CAKE; 12 SLICES

Baked Carrot Pudding

FOOD VALUES	TOTAL	PER PORTION
Protein	66g	11g
Carbohydrate	374g	62g
Fat	133g	22g
Fibre	26g	4g
kcals	2866	477

350 g / 12 oz carrots, thinly sliced
oil for greasing
225 g / 8 oz fresh wholemeal breadcrumbs
100 g / 4 oz raisins
100 g / 4 oz currants
75 g / 3 oz soft light brown sugar
100 g / 4 oz shredded suet
5 ml / 1 tsp grated nutmeg
3 eggs, beaten
about 450 ml / ¾ pint milk, see method
caster sugar to sprinkle

Cook the carrots in boiling water for about 15 minutes, until tender. Drain and mash them thoroughly until smooth.

Set the oven at 180°C / 350°F / gas 4. Grease a 1.4 litre / 2½ pint ovenproof dish – a large pie dish or gratin dish is ideal, but not a deep soufflé dish. Mix the breadcrumbs, raisins, currants, sugar, suet and nutmeg in a large bowl. Add the carrots and eggs, and mix well until all the ingredients are thoroughly combined. Add enough milk to give the mixture the consistency of a thick batter.

Turn the mixture into the dish and smooth the top. Bake for 1½-1¾ hours, until set and golden on top. Sprinkle with a little caster sugar. Serve hot or warm.

SERVES 6

Mrs Beeton's Potato Fritters

A recipe to reserve for an occasional family treat – these fritters are very light and easily eaten in quantity with the complementary sherry sauce. The secret of success when cooking them is to keep the oil at just the right temperature.

FOOD VALUES	TOTAL	PER PORTION (6)
Protein	37g	6g
Carbohydrate	126g	21g
Fat	38g	6g
Fibre	7g	1g
kcals	1213	202

450 g / 1 lb potatoes, boiled
 and mashed
40 g / 1½ oz plain flour
3 eggs
30 ml / 2 tbsp double cream
30 ml / 2 tbsp cream sherry
10 ml / 2 tsp lemon juice
2.5 ml / ½ tsp grated
 nutmeg
oil for deep frying
caster sugar for dredging

SHERRY SAUCE
200 ml / 7 fl oz sweet sherry
juice of 1 lemon, strained
sugar to taste

Rub the mashed potatoes through a sieve placed over a bowl, to remove any lumps. Beat in the flour, then gradually beat in the eggs, cream, sherry, lemon juice and nutmeg. Continue to beat the batter until it is extremely smooth and light.

Heat the oil for frying in a deep wide saucepan to 180°C / 350°F or until a bread cube immersed in the oil turns pale brown in 45 seconds. Use two dessertspoons to drop small portions of batter into the oil and fry for about 1 minute, until puffed and golden. Drain well on absorbent kitchen paper and dredge with caster sugar. Keep hot under a warm grill until all the batter is cooked.

Meanwhile, warm the sherry and lemon juice in a small saucepan. Stir in sugar to taste. Pour into a jug. Serve the fritters with the warmed sherry sauce.

SERVES 6 TO 8

Potato Pudding

FOOD V.	TOTAL	PER PORTION (4)
Protei	24g	6g
Carbon	101g	25g
Fat	60g	15g
Fibre	3g	1g
kcals	1064	266

butter for greasing
225 g / 8 oz freshly cooked and mashed potato
50 g / 2 oz butter
150 ml / ¼ pint milk
45 ml / 3 tbsp sherry
1.25 ml / ¼ tsp salt
grated rind and juice of 2 lemons
50 g / 2 oz sugar
2 eggs, beaten

Grease a 1.1 litre / 2 pint pie dish with butter. Set the oven at 190°C / 375°F / gas 5. Beat the potatoes well to ensure they are smooth, then gradually add the butter, milk, sherry and salt and mix well. Mix in the lemon rind and juice with the sugar and the beaten eggs.

Turn the mixture into the prepared pie dish and bake for about 45 minutes, until set and lightly browned. Serve at once.

SERVES 4 TO 6

MRS BEETON'S TIP

Potato pudding has a pleasing, delicate flavour and a smooth texture. The 'mashed-potato-like' texture may not be to everyone's liking but the pudding can be given a slightly more 'spongy' consistency by adding 50 g / 2 oz fresh white breadcrumbs with the milk and sherry.

Marrow Pudding

FOOD VALUES	TOTAL	PER PORTION
Protein	73g	12g
Carbohydrate	249g	42g
Fat	67g	11g
Fibre	4g	1g
kcals	1830	305

oil for greasing
100 g / 4 oz fresh
  breadcrumbs
900 ml / 1½ pints milk
175 g / 6 oz peeled and
  seeded marrow
4 eggs, beaten
100 g / 4 oz raisins or
  currants, or 50 g / 2 oz
  of each
75 g / 3 oz sugar
caster sugar to sprinkle

Grease a 1.4 litre / 2½ pint soufflé dish. Place the breadcrumbs in a large heatproof bowl. Bring the milk to the boil, pour it over the breadcrumbs, cover and leave to stand for 30 minutes.

Coarsely grate the marrow and add it to the breadcrumb mixture with the eggs, raisins or currants and sugar. Mix well to ensure the ingredients are thoroughly combined, then turn the mixture into the prepared dish. Bake for about 1½ hours, until golden and set. Sprinkle with a little caster sugar before serving hot.

SERVES 6

PRESERVES

Pickled Onions

This is a recipe for onions without tears. Soaking the unskinned onions in brine makes them easy to peel.

450 g / 1 lb salt
1.4 kg / 3 lb pickling onions
2.25 litres / 4 pints cold
  Spiced Vinegar, (see Mrs
  Beeton's Tip, page 49)
5 ml / 1 tsp mustard seeds
  (optional)

Dissolve half the salt in 2 litres / 3½ pints of water in a large bowl. Add the onions. Set a plate inside the bowl to keep the onions submerged, weighting the plate with a jar filled with water. Do not use a can as the salt water would corrode it. Leave for 24 hours.

Drain and skin the onions and return them to the clean bowl. Make up a fresh solution of brine, using the rest of the salt and a further 2 litres / 3½ pints water. Pour it over the onions, weight as before and leave for a further 24 hours. Drain the onions, rinse them thoroughly to remove excess salt, and drain again. Pack into wide-mouthed jars. Cover with cold spiced vinegar, adding a few mustard seeds to each jar, if liked. Cover with vinegar-proof lids. Label and store in a cool, dark place. Keep for at least 1 month before using.

MAKES ABOUT 1.4 KG / 3 LB

NOTE

Food values are not given for the vegetables pickled in vinegar but they are provided for preserves such as chutney and jam, where the portion size is estimated at 15 ml / 1 tbsp.

Pickled Red Cabbage

Do not make too much of this pickle at one time, as it will lose its crispness if stored for longer than two or three months.

1 *firm red cabbage*
100-150 *g / 4-5 oz salt*
2-3 *onions, very thinly sliced*
soft dark brown sugar
  (*see method*)
600-900 *ml / 1-1½ pints*
  Spiced Vinegar (see Mrs
  Beeton's Tip, page 149)

Remove any discoloured outer leaves from the cabbage, cut it into quarters and then into shreds. Layer the shreds in a large bowl, sprinkling each layer with salt. Cover the bowl and leave overnight. Next day, rinse the cabbage and drain it very thoroughly in a colander, pressing out all the surplus liquid.

Pack a 7.5 cm / 3 inch layer of cabbage in a large glass jar. Cover with a layer of onion and sprinkle with 5 ml / 1 tsp brown sugar. Repeat the layers until the jar is full, using additional jars if necessary. Fill the jar or jars with spiced vinegar. Cover with vinegar-proof lids. Label and store in a cool, dark place. Keep for at least 1 week before using.

MAKES ABOUT 1.4 KG / 3 LB

Pickled Beetroot

1.4 *kg / 3 lb beetroot*
600-750 *ml / 1-1¼ pints*
  Spiced Vinegar (see Mrs
  Beeton's Tip, page 149)
15-20 *g / ½-¾ oz salt*

Set the oven at 180°C / 350°F / gas 4. Wash the beetroot thoroughly but gently, taking care not to break the skin. Place in a roasting tin and bake for 45-60 minutes or until tender. Cool, then skin and cube. Pour the spiced vinegar into a saucepan, add the salt and bring to the boil.

Meanwhile, pack the beetroot cubes into wide-mouthed jars. Cover with boiling vinegar and put on vinegar-proof covers. Seal, label and store in a cool, dark place for 3 months before eating.

MAKES ABOUT 1.4 KG / 3 LB

Mixed Pickle

When garden and greenhouse are bursting with new young vegetables, it is a good idea to pickle some of the surplus. For this versatile recipe any of the following can be used: small cucumbers, cauliflower, baby onions, small French beans. Only the onions need to be peeled; everything else should merely be cut into suitably sized pieces.

1 kg / 2¼ lb prepared mixed vegetables
50 g / 2 oz cooking salt
600-750 ml / 1-1¼ pints Spiced Vinegar (see Mrs Beeton's Tip, right)

Put all the vegetables in a large bowl, sprinkle with the salt, cover and leave for 24 hours.

Rinse, drain thoroughly, then pack into jars. Cover with cold spiced vinegar and seal with vinegar-proof covers. Store in a cool, dark place for at least 1 month before using.

MAKES ABOUT 1 KG / 2¼ LB

MRS BEETON'S TIP

A variety of covers are vinegar-proof and thus suitable for pickles and chutneys. The most obvious choice are the twist-top or screw-on plastic-coated lids used commercially. Press-on plastic covers are also suitable. Alternatively, cut a circle of clean card or paper to the size of the top of the jar. Set it in place and cover with a piece of linen dipped in melted paraffin wax. Tie the linen firmly in place.

Pickled Gherkins

Small cucumbers known as dills or gherkins require longer
processing than most other vegetables.

25 (7.5 cm / 3 inch) dill
  cucumbers
cooking salt (see method)
600 ml / 1 pint Spiced
  Vinegar (see Mrs Beeton's
  Tip, below)
4-6 garlic cloves, peeled
4-6 dill sprigs

Select dill cucumbers / gherkins of the same size.
Put them in a saucepan and cover with a solution of
brine made in the proportion of 225 g / 8 oz salt to 2
litres / 3½ pints water. Bring the liquid to just below
boiling point, lower the temperature and simmer
for 10 minutes. Drain and leave until cold, then pack
into clean jars and cover with spiced vinegar. Add 1
garlic clove and 1 dill sprig to each jar. Seal with
vinegar-proof covers, label the jars and store in a
cool, dark place.

MAKES ABOUT 1.4 KG / 3 LB

MRS BEETON'S TIP

To make 1 litre / 1¾ pints of Spiced Vinegar you will need 7 g / ¼ oz each of
cloves, allspice berries, broken cinnamon sticks and fresh root ginger (bruised)
plus 1 litre / 1¾ pints white or malt vinegar. Fold the spices in a clean cloth.
Using a rolling pin, beat lightly to release all the flavour. Combine the spices
and vinegar in a large jug, mix well, then pour the liquid into a 1.1 litre / 2 pint
bottle; seal tightly. Shake the bottle daily for 1 month, then store in a cool dry
place for at least 1 month more before straining out the spices and returning
the vinegar to the clean bottle.

Marrow and Ginger Jam

FOOD VALUES	TOTAL	PER PORTION
Protein	8g	–
Carbohydrate	1637g	9g
Fat	3g	–
Fibre	8g	–
kcals	6199	35

1.5 kg / 3¼ lb marrow,
   peeled and cut up
2 lemons
100 g / 4 oz crystallized
   ginger, cut up
1.5 kg / 3¼ lb sugar

Put the marrow in a metal colander set over a saucepan of boiling water, cover the marrow with the pan lid and steam for 10-20 minutes or until tender. Drain thoroughly and mash to a pulp.

Meanwhile, grate the rind from the lemons, squeeze out the juice and place both in a small saucepan. Chop the remaining lemon shells and tie them in muslin. Add the muslin bag to the lemon mixture and pour in just enough water to cover. Bring to the boil, lower the heat and cover the pan. Simmer for 30 minutes. Squeeze the bag and boil the liquid, without the lid on the pan, until reduced to the original volume of lemon juice.

Combine the marrow, ginger and lemon liquid in a preserving pan. Bring to the boil, add the sugar, then stir over low heat until dissolved. Boil until the setting point is reached. Remove from the heat, skim, pot, cover and label.

MAKES ABOUT 2.5 KG / 5½ LB

MRS BEETON'S TIP
This jam will not produce a definite set; it should be potted when it reaches the desired volume and consistency.

Carrot Preserve

Mrs Beeton's carrot jam was intended to imitate apricot preserve. Sampled in ignorance, the association between carrots and this smooth, pleasant-tasting preserve is not immediately apparent. Adding the whole of the lemon, instead of the rind alone, gives the cooked pulp a better consistency.

FOOD VALUES	TOTAL	PER PORTION
Protein	11g	—
Carbohydrate	784g	8g
Fat	17g	—
Fibre	24g	—
kcals	3271	34

2 large lemons
900 g / 2 lb carrots, sliced
5 ml / 1 tsp oil of bitter almonds or natural almond flavouring
25 g / 1 oz blanched almonds, chopped
675 g / 1½ lb sugar
60 ml / 4 tbsp brandy

Wash, dry and grate the lemons. Squeeze out the juice and reserve with the rind. Finely chop the shells and place them in a small saucepan. Pour in just enough water to cover the lemon. Bring to the boil, cover tightly, lower the heat and simmer for about 1 hour or until the pulp is soft. Strain the cooking liquid through a fine sieve into a jug; set aside.

Cook the carrots in a saucepan of boiling water until tender, then drain and mash. Place the mashed carrots in a preserving pan. Add the grated lemon rind and juice, strained cooking liquid, almond oil or flavouring and nuts. Add the sugar and heat gently, stirring all the time until the sugar has dissolved completely.

Bring to the boil and boil rapidly until setting point is reached. Remove from the heat and skim. Stir in the brandy, pot, cover and label.

MAKES ABOUT 1.4 KG / 3 LB

Pumpkin Preserve

Originally, Mrs Beeton advised cutting the pumpkin into pieces
about the size of a 'five-shilling piece'. This recipe may also
be used for marrow and, of course, it may be doubled, trebled or
increased according to the weight of pumpkin flesh you have to
preserve. Do not do more than double the ginger
or it will be overpowering.

FOOD VALUES	TOTAL	PER PORTION
Protein	4g	–
Carbohydrate	485g	5g
Fat	1g	–
Fibre	5g	–
kcals	1842	19

450 g / 1 lb pumpkin flesh
450 g / 1 lb sugar
2.5 cm / 1 inch fresh root
ginger, sliced
grated rind of 1 lemon
150 ml / ¼ pint lemon juice

The pumpkin should be weighed after peeling and
discarding the seeds. Cut the flesh into 2.5 cm /
1 inch cubes. Layer them in a large bowl, sprinkling
each layer with sugar, ginger slices and grated
lemon rind. Pour the lemon juice over, cover the
bowl and leave to stand for 2-3 days, stirring
occasionally.

Turn the pumpkin into a large preserving pan,
scraping in all the juices from the bowl. Add 100
ml / 3½ fl oz water. Bring to the boil, stirring, then
lower the heat and simmer for 30-40 minutes, until
the pumpkin is tender but not reduced to a pulp.
Stir occasionally.

Spoon the pumpkin and juices into a bowl, cover
and leave in a cold place for 1 week, stirring every
day. Strain the syrup into a saucepan, adding the
ginger slices from the strainer. Pack the pumpkin
into jars. Bring the syrup mixture to the boil and
boil until reduced by half. Pour the boiling syrup
over the pumpkin, cover and label.

MAKES ABOUT 1.4 KG / 3 LB

FREEZING VEGETABLES

All vegetables should be young, fresh and clean, and frozen as soon as possible after picking. Open freeze blanched vegetables, then pack them in free-flow packs so that small quantities can be removed as required. Vegetables should be cooked from frozen. Since they are blanched they cook quickly; however the time taken to thaw them means that the overall cooking time is about the same, or slightly less, than for fresh produce. Add the frozen vegetables to boiling water, steam them or toss them in hot butter, according to type.

PREPARING VEGETABLES FOR FREEZING

All raw vegetables should be prepared as for cooking. Produce should be trimmed, washed and dried. The majority of vegetables should be blanched.

Blanching

Vegetables benefit from blanching. Enzymes, naturally present in the food, cause it to ripen, then eventually to become overripe and finally to rot. During freezing, enzyme activity is slowed down considerably but it is not fully halted; in some vegetables, therefore, the produce may deteriorate in quality if stored for long periods.

The enzymes are destroyed by exposure to temperatures equal to those of boiling water for a short period of time (this varies according to the food and enzyme). Blanching vegetables destroys the enzymes and improves the keeping quality during freezing.

However, if vegetables are to be frozen for short periods (2-4 weeks), there is no need to blanch them. Some vegetables keep well for far longer periods without blanching; others deteriorate rapidly, developing off flavours. This is particularly true of broad beans, which should always be blanched if storing for longer than 2 weeks.

Blanching Method

To prevent food from being cooked during blanching it is important that it is placed in rapidly boiling water, which is brought back to the boil as quickly as possible, then drained immediately. To facilitate speedy cooling, the drained food should be immersed in iced water. This prevents continued cooking by residual heat.

Blanch manageable quantities at a time – if large batches are processed the water takes longer to come back to the boil and the vegetables tend to cook rather than remain crisp and / or firm.

Have ready a large saucepan, a wire basket and a large bowl (or thoroughly clean sink) of iced water. Place the prepared vegetables in the basket and plunge them into the boiling water. Bring the water back to the boil, then time

the blanching exactly. Remove the vegetables and plunge them straight into iced water as soon as the required time is reached. Drain well, pat dry on absorbent kitchen paper, then pack the vegetables and freeze.

PACKING FRESH VEGETABLES FOR FREEZING

To avoid the development of cross-flavours between foods in the freezer and to prevent deterioration in quality, it is essential that all vegetables be adequately packed.

Packing Materials These must be waterproof; they should form an airtight seal when closed. Plastics, whether containers or bags, are ideal. Although foil keeps moisture in, it tends to be too fragile and tears easily.

Sheets of plastic tissue may be used for interleaving stacked items, such as chops or burgers.

Bags should be heavy gauge; thin ones do not keep in moisture, nor do they prevent exposure to the air from causing the food to dry out.

Freezer Burn This results from poor packing: the surface of the food dries out and looks pale. It is caused by dehydration and is not remedied on thawing and cooking.

Open Freezing This is a useful technique for some prepared vegetables, such as sliced green beans which will otherwise freeze in a solid block, and other individual items which are best frozen separately. The food should be prepared, then spread out on trays lined with freezer film or foil. The trays should then be placed in the freezer until the food is hard, and the items subsequently packed in airtight bags. This allows large quantities to be packed in a single bag, and because the items are free-flowing, small amounts may be removed for cooking as required.

Removing Air It is important to remove air from freezer packs as it is a factor in the formation of freezer burn. To displace the air, the pack of food may be immersed in a bowl of water. Once all air has been removed, the opening should be sealed with a wire tie. The exterior of the pack should be dried before freezing.

Labelling Always label packs of food with details of the food or dish, the date and any notes about potential use.

FREEZING COOKED VEGETABLE DISHES

Cooked vegetables are not as universally successful for freezing as raw produce. However many cooked dishes containing vegetables are excellent freezer candidates. The following are a few pointers worth remembering.

- Plain cooked vegetables, such as carrots, beans, peas and boiled potatoes, become watery and soft textured on thawing.
- Cooked and mashed vegetables freeze well. Potatoes, carrots, parsnips, celeriac and swede may all be frozen when mashed with a little butter or margarine. Beat well after thawing.
- Mushrooms, carrots and other vegetables added to casseroles become watery on thawing. It is best to freeze meat casseroles without these ingredients and to add them (freshly cooked) after thawing.
- Vegetable soups and smooth sauces freeze well. Do not add cream, yogurt, eggs or other ingredients which may curdle during freezing; incorporate these ingredients with the soup or sauce after thawing and reheating.
- Some comparatively dry cooked dishes containing vegetables freeze reasonably well – pies, pasties and vegetable burgers or bakes, such as moussaka are typical examples.
- As for any cooked dishes, vegetable dishes for freezing should be cooled and chilled as soon as possible after cooking; then wrapped and frozen promptly.
- The storage life of *any* cooked dish is only as long as the shortest storage time for individual ingredients it contains.

USING FROZEN VEGETABLES AND VEGETABLE DISHES

Vegetables should be cooked from frozen. Composite dishes such as casseroles and bakes should be thawed before use.

Thawing Food The safest way to thaw a frozen composite vegetable dish is to unwrap it and place it in a covered container in the refrigerator overnight.

The important point to remember is that as the food thaws, the bacteria and enzymes contained in it slowly become active as the temperature rises. While the food remains very cold there is no risk of it being open to contamination by bacterial growth; however if the food is left in a warm room for a long period, parts, if not all, of it will become sufficiently warm for bacteria to grow. Foods left in this manner for long periods may develop high levels of bacteria with the possible consequence of food poisoning.

It is therefore vital that any food thawed at room temperature should be frequently monitored. It should be used as soon as it is thawed, while still cold.

VEGETABLE FREEZING CHART

Type of vegetable	Preparation for freezing	Blanching time	High quality storage life
Artichokes (globe)	Remove outer leaves, stalks, and chokes. Add lemon juice to blanching water.	7 minutes	12 months
Artichokes (Jerusalem)	Peel and slice. Cook and purée.	–	3 months
Asparagus	Trim and cut in lengths.	2 minutes (thin) 3 minutes (medium) 4 minutes (large)	9 months
Avocados	Mash pulp with lemon juice (15 ml / 1 tbsp juice to each avocado).	–	1 month
Beans (broad)	Shell small young beans.	1½ minutes	12 months
Beans (French)	Top and tail young beans. Leave whole or cut into 2 cm / ¾ inch chunks.	3 minutes (whole) 2 minutes (cut)	12 months
Beans (runner)	Cut as preferred.	2 minutes	12 months
Beetroot	Cook very young beet, under 2.5 cm / 1 inch in diameter. Peel and leave whole.	–	6 months
Broccoli	Trim stalks and soak in brine for 30 minutes. Wash before blanching.	3 minutes (thin) 4 minutes (medium) 5 minutes (thick)	12 months
Brussels sprouts	Trim and prepare for cooking.	3 minutes (small) 4 minutes (medium)	12 months
Carrots	Use very young carrots. Wash and scrape. Leave whole, dice or slice.	3 minutes	12 months
Cauliflower	Wash and break into florets. Add lemon juice to blanching water.	3 minutes	6 months

VEGETABLE FREEZING CHART

Type of vegetable	Preparation for freezing	Blanching time	High quality storage life
Corn on the cob	Use fresh tender corn. Remove husks and silks.	4 minutes (small) 6 minutes (medium) 8 minutes (large)	12 months
Courgettes	Cut courgettes into 1 cm / ½ inch slices without peeling.	3 minutes	2 months
Herbs	Wash and pack whole sprigs or chop.	–	6 months
Leeks	Clean and cut into rings.	2 minutes	12 months
Mushrooms	Wipe but do not peel. Pack or open freeze without blanching.	–	3 months
Onions	Skin and chop or slice. Double wrap.	2 minutes	2 months
Parsnips, turnips, and swedes	Peel and dice.	2 minutes	12 months
Peas	Shell young sweet peas.	1 minute	12 months
Peppers	Remove seeds and membranes.	3 minutes (halves) 2 minutes (slices)	12 months
Potatoes	Cook and mash, or make into croquettes. Jacket, baked and roast potatoes can be frozen. Fry chips for 4 minutes but do not brown.	–	3 months
Spinach	Remove any stalks and wash leaves very well. Press out moisture after blanching.	2 minutes	12 months
Tomatoes	Purée and pack in rigid containers.	–	12 months

INDEX

158